THE TEB MODEL

THE TEB MODEL

A New Approach to Crisis Assessment and Intervention

John Azar-Dickens, PhD

BOOKLOGIX®
Alpharetta, Georgia

The resources contained within this book are provided for informational purposes only and should not be used to replace the specialized training and professional judgment of a healthcare or mental healthcare professional. Reading this book does not establish a therapist-client, psychologist-patient, or any other professional relationship between the reader and the author. Author and the publisher of this work cannot be held responsible for the use of the information provided. Always consult a licensed mental health professional before making any decision regarding treatment of yourself or others.

Copyright © 2025 by John Azar-Dickens

All rights reserved. No part of this book may be reproduced or transmitted in any form or by any means, electronic or mechanical, including photocopying, recording, or any information storage and retrieval system, without permission in writing from the author.

ISBN: 978-1-6653-1022-2 - Paperback
eISBN: 978-1-6653-1023-9 - eBook

These ISBNs are the property of BookLogix for the express purpose of sales and distribution of this title. The content of this book is the property of the copyright holder only. BookLogix does not hold any ownership of the content of this book and is not liable in any way for the materials contained within. The views and opinions expressed in this book are the property of the Author/Copyright holder, and do not necessarily reflect those of BookLogix.

Library of Congress Control Number: 2025908635

☉This paper meets the requirements of ANSI/NISO Z39.48-1992 (Permanence of Paper)

1 0 2 4 2 5

This book is dedicated to the men and women of law enforcement—the brave souls who put on the uniform, leave their homes and families each and every day, and put their lives on the line in service to the community. May we never forget their commitment and sacrifice.

In the midst of every crisis lies great opportunity.
  —Albert Einstein

CONTENTS

Preface   xi
Introduction   xv

CHAPTER I: THE HISTORY AND FOUNDATION OF TEB   1
    Rationale for Development   1
    Mental Health Diagnostic Labels   3
    What the TEB Is   6
    What the TEB Is Not   7
    What Is a Crisis?   8
    The Fluidity of TEB   9
    How TEB Can Be Used   9
    The SOAAR Model   10

CHAPTER II: INSTRUMENT CONTENT   15
    Thought   15
    Emotion   19
    Behavior   20
    The TEB Profiles   23
    Approach Style   23
    Psychological Status   28
    Volatility Risk   28
    Volatility Type   29
    Other Behavioral Factors to Consider   29

CHAPTER III: ANALYSIS AND CLINICAL EXAMPLES   31
    Contaminated Thought–High Emotion–
       Compliant Behavior   31
    Contaminated Thought–High Emotion–
       Noncompliant Behavior   37

Contaminated Thought–Low Emotion– Compliant Behavior	44
Contaminated Thought–Low Emotion– Noncompliant Behavior	49
Clear Thought–High Emotion– Compliant Behavior	55
Clear Thought–High Emotion– Noncompliant Behavior	60
Clear Thought–Low Emotion– Compliant Behavior	65
Clear Thought–Low Emotion– Noncompliant Behavior	68
CHAPTER IV: APPLICATION FOR THE POLICE TRAINER	73
Three Phases of TEB Application	75
Conclusion	*79*
Bibliography	*81*

PREFACE

As I entered the room, I could see him there. The subject, sitting quietly on a bed, head in his hands. Around the room lay the broken items he had destroyed during his emotional tirade. But now, he sat quietly, unresponsive and unwilling to engage. Around him stood four officers, blankly staring at each other, with no clear plan on how to move forward. They were faced with an unpredictable male who had, just moments earlier, been aggressive and disruptive. However, now, he was sitting quietly and refusing to engage in any interaction. These were four highly skilled officers who were eager to engage him and address the challenges he was facing. However, the problem was they had no idea what they were dealing with and therefore no strategy for how to communicate with him.

While the officers' training had exposed them to various mental health diagnostic labels and introduced them to the suffering of those with mental health conditions, what they were not prepared for was how to quickly assess what was in front of them, and based on that assessment, how to develop a strategy for communication. Their training had failed to provide a structured means by which to assess an individual and thereby build a communication strategy.

Traditional police training has emphasized a model of communication that is directive in nature and applied to everyone in the same manner. First you ask, then you tell, and then you make. The issue of noncompliance is seen as a volitional maneuver that is a result of disdain for our authority, and as such, we must force compliance. More recently, the concept of "de-escalation" has infiltrated law enforcement. The tide has shifted and now officers are told they must use de-escalation during subject interaction, especially if it is "assumed" the person is having some type of "mental health crisis." This is translated in practice to things like creating space, slowing things down, and using active listening strategies.

While there is certainly value in directive communication for some folks and de-escalation for others, the question becomes, how are officers to know which is best and for whom? It is not at all surprising these officers were uncertain how to communicate with the individual in this room. When you use broad terms like "mental health crisis" and "de-escalation," nobody really knows what that all means. It certainly does not provide an operational foundation for making decisions about how to communicate and intervene.

As I watched the officers struggling to understand how to address the needs of the man sitting before them, it occurred to me that there is a significant piece missing from our police training. Officers are quite skilled in communicating with subjects, with skills they have developed through training and experience, but the gap seems to be in quick assessment. It is the assessment of the person that drives decision-making about intervention, and without it, the officer is left with little clarity on what to do or say. Absence of assessment skills results in a one-intervention-fits-all model that is heavily flawed and fails to consider the numerous motivations and issues that drive human functioning. It also raises the risk of choosing the wrong intervention strategy which creates a greater risk for intervention failure, potentially escalates the individual, and/or places the officer in greater jeopardy. However, the use of mental health labels for rapid assessment is of limited value and provides nothing in the way of a foundation for intervention. This is because we not only can't diagnose on the street, but as will be discussed later, mental health diagnosis was not created for the purpose of dealing with a person in crisis.

This all brought me to a question. If I don't believe mental health labels should be the focus of the officer deciding how to intervene with a subject, what should be the focus? In other words, when an officer encounters a subject, where should their attention be directed? Certainly, tactical awareness is always paramount and should be a consideration throughout the time with an individual. But, what else?

As I thought deeply about this, I fell back on my training as a psychologist regarding what is important for me to address. As a psychologist, when someone enters the office, what is my focus in assessing the problem? In addition, for the police officer on the street, this assessment needs to happen quickly, as there is often little time for contemplation and analysis. Officers operate in uncertain environments, with variable boundaries, limited structure, limited time, and a much greater level of unpredictability than is afforded a psychologist. As such, there needs to be an approach officers can use that considers their unique circumstances, while still providing a solid means for proper assessment and intervention.

The answer is the focus should be on the fundamental

elements of human functioning. Specifically, what we as humans do all day, which involves thinking, emoting, and behaving. It is these core areas of human functioning that provide the essential information we need to make decisions on what is happening with an individual, and in response, what is the best way for us to intervene and communicate with this person in achieving our police objective. This doesn't require advanced clinical knowledge, memorization of various disorders and symptoms, or any advanced training in psychopathology. Rather, it is a simple and quick analysis of what is in front of us as a means of acquiring a foundation for our interventions.

In addition to recognizing various profiles that help us identify when a person is in crisis, it is also important for us to recognize when a person is not. Many an officer has been hurt or killed trying to utilize "de-escalation strategies" with the wrong person. While it is imperative that we communicate with individuals in crisis with a very specific type of communication that is designed to de-escalate, we must also have the wherewithal to know when this type of communication can be to our detriment and potentially allow someone to use it to their benefit.

The thought-emotion-behavior (TEB) model is a culmination of what I have learned as both a psychologist and a police officer, with an attempt to integrate the best of both worlds. It incorporates sound clinical judgment within a realistic framework that can be easily applied within the oftentimes chaotic world in which an officer operates. It is also designed to be easily acquired and is void of complicated clinical jargon and "psychobabble" that can often lead us down a rabbit hole of useless information.

INTRODUCTION

In 2012, noted researchers Dr. Joan Vickers and Dr. William Lewinski joined forces to research the gaze control, decision-making, and shooting performance of elite versus rookie police officers. The focus of this research was to understand the tactical performance differences between rookie and elite officers. This study revealed fascinating information related to our most elite officers and helped us understand what is important to focus on during a tactical encounter so that performance can be optimized.

This research added valuable information to help inform trainers about how to develop the most effective skills an officer needs for tactical excellence. When a threat presents itself, we want our officers to be highly skilled and prepared to immediately, safely, and effectively neutralize a threat.

The job of a police officer requires constant training and preparation for handling dangerous threats. We spend hours training defensive tactics, firearms, and other skills in readiness for the threats inherent to our world today. The public expects police officers to be trained and ready to answer the call, to run toward the threat, and neutralize the danger when it emerges.

Unfortunately, this level of training and the depth of information available to police officers related to a person in crisis doesn't appear to rise to the same level of excellence offered in neutralizing a dangerous threat. For instance, if you were to ask an officer, "What is your strategy for handling that dangerous person?" an officer is likely to provide you with a litany of tactical strategies they might employ to quickly intervene and stop the threat. However, if you were to ask that same officer, "What is your strategy to address this person in crisis?" the response would likely be far less detailed.

The disparity that exists between these two areas of knowledge and practical application is not the fault of the officer. Rather, it is the result of limited information available to the policing profession in general as applied to a person in crisis. Our training as this is concerned tends to be fairly generic, with some general education about various mental illnesses, education about active listening, and vague commandments to "slow things down," create space, and essentially "be nice to the person." De-escalation training in most departments is far less comprehensive and detailed when compared with the tactical elements of training. In many areas, education about dealing with a person in crisis boils down to "do what you can, but just don't use force." While these types of things may resonate with some, it does little to provide practical, concrete, realistic, officer-safety-focused information officers need to address a person in crisis.

Much of the problem has been in trying to apply a monolithic approach to crisis management. Specifically, to try to frame all of the potential issues that can drive a crisis situation through a lens of mental illness. In simpler terms, to try to generalize the knowledge base and skills of a mental health practitioner to the work of a police officer.

When I decided to become a police officer, I had to attend an academy for training. I couldn't just walk out of my office as a trained psychologist and do the job of a police officer. The skill set is very different than that of a psychologist. Just ask my field training officer, who routinely told me I was going to get killed if I didn't stop "thinking like a psychologist." While my specific skill set as a psychologist had merit, it was designed to be applied in situations where there was information, time, structure, boundaries, and predictability. When someone in a hospital setting was in a crisis state, I had four walls as a boundary, large orderlies to handle any necessary force, and a whole lot of pharmaceuticals to use that could quickly put an end to the crisis. When I found myself behind the local shop and rob at 2 a.m. with an intoxicated man in crisis as a police officer, that was a whole different ball game. There were no orderlies, no medications, no walls, no information, and very little time. Granted, there were other officers available for support, but the playing field was entirely different.

While the specific skills and education of a mental health practitioner certainly have merit and the police discipline can benefit from integrating this knowledge base into our police practice, it is not cleanly generalizable and there are many flaws. The trick is taking the useful information and integrating it into a practice and skill set that is appropriate for the highly dynamic, rapidly changing, unpredictable world the police officer must work within. In other words, we need our own unique crisis-management tactics applicable to our world rather than a watered-down, poorly generalizable system designed for an entirely different playing field.

The development of TEB is my attempt to offer this. It is the application of psychological science and our understanding of fundamental elements of human existence into a format that is easy to learn and quick to apply, while also keeping intact the necessary tactical awareness that is essential for officer safety. It is a model of assessment and intervention that is uniquely designed for the law enforcement officer who is tasked with providing support, direction, and management of people in crisis within a very dynamic playing field.

The focus of this book is to dive deeply into the thought-emotion-behavior approach of subject assessment and intervention. It begins with a history of the development of the TEB model. In essence, an understanding of why I believe this type of approach is necessary and how it can enhance officer performance with people in crisis.

We then explore the specific structural foundation of the model itself. Individual concepts of thought, emotion, and behavior are explored, with information as to how each is evaluated within the model. Additional categories within the model itself are also addressed specifically, with illustrations and explanations of each.

The book dives deeply into exploring each of the eight TEB profiles, providing in-depth analysis, clinical examples, possible psychological conditions driving the individual profile, suggestions to consider for intervention, and other important information.

The end of the book provides valuable information to police trainers who are tasked with the job of training crisis management to officers. I offer suggestions for applying the TEB model in a training setting, in a manner that involves not only education related to the material, but also practical application through high-fidelity training.

This book is written primarily for a law enforcement audience. However, other disciplines may find the TEB model interesting for their own unique needs. This would include mental health co-responders and clinicians who are attached to various patrol units and are responsible for providing support to officers in addressing the needs of a person in crisis. Mental health practitioners involved in law enforcement education may also consider this model a useful tool in their educational toolkit.

The TEB model is a theoretical model grounded in psychological science. This book is only the beginning of what I hope will be rigorous research, analysis, and continued development of comprehensive information related to crisis management that is realistic for officers and easily integrated into their complex skill set. More importantly, it is information I hope will not only enhance the already exceptional skills officers demonstrate each and every day, but also add another layer to officer safety so that each can come home to their families at the end of every shift.

CHAPTER I

THE HISTORY AND FOUNDATION OF TEB

The TEB Model is a theoretical model designed to aid officers in rapid psychological assessment as a means of making an informed decision as it relates to communication and influence during a police encounter on the street. It provides officers with a tangible model to focus attention on critical key issues of subject functioning, to then build upon in making decisions about how best to intervene and achieve their police objectives. With increased awareness of these elements, officers can then make rapid and functional decisions about how best to influence and persuade subjects.

RATIONALE FOR DEVELOPMENT

In training for line officers related to influence and persuasion of challenging subjects, the focus has been either directed toward traditional police tactics or solely on mental health diagnosis. This dichotomy says to officers either use your traditional tactics or, if you think the person might be mentally ill based on behaviors associated with some type of mental illness, do something different. The issue of a "subject in crisis" is often presented to line officers within the context of traditional psychiatric diagnostic labels, with some later discussions around how to best address the needs of these individuals. This typically comes within the context of de-escalation training and offers a cursory view of psychiatric diagnosis. This is a concern in that very few psychiatric conditions actually follow traditional symptom presentation on the street, and people who are in a crisis situation may not have any specific psychiatric disorder. In fact, many of the subjects officers encounter who are in crisis do not have a mental illness at all. There is also considerable crossover of symptoms within psychiatric diagnosis, making an accurate diagnosis difficult, even for those who are trained to do it professionally. For example, consider a symptom of inattention. If someone is inattentive, what diagnosis do they have? Well, the answer to that is they could have many. There are numerous diagnoses that have inattention as a symptom, and to narrow down specifically what the correct diagnosis is would require background information, behavioral observation over time, medical testing, psychological testing, and a myriad of other pieces of data to try to understand. The use of mental health labeling as the foundation for officer decision-making related to how to intervene with a subject is flawed and provides little in the way of a solid, reliable solution. Therefore, it becomes crucial for officers to develop the ability to quickly assess a subject without relying on diagnostic labeling, and to do so in a manner that provides quick data from which to make decisions. This would be the case regardless of whether a person suffers from a mental illness.

MENTAL HEALTH DIAGNOSTIC LABELS

The definition of a mental illness as defined by the American Psychiatric Association is as follows:

> A mental illness is a syndrome that involves significant disturbance in a person's behavior, cognition, emotion regulation, or behavior that reflects a dysfunction in the psychological, biological, or developmental processes underlying mental functioning. (2022)

This definition indicates that a mental illness is essentially a dysfunction or disturbance in the thought, emotion, and/or behavior of an individual. This disturbance could impact one specific area, such as a profound impact on emotional functioning, or be more severe and impact all three areas simultaneously. With the use of TEB, the goal is to go directly to the foundational elements of mental health labels rather than using the labels themselves.

Psychiatric diagnosis has three main purposes. First, it allows for easy communication between clinicians by providing a label that immediately suggests a specific pattern of symptoms. Second, it allows for the development of empirically supported therapy and medication treatments. Last, it provides a framework for research to be done in order to accurately measure the effectiveness of treatment interventions. These diagnostic labels were not developed for police encounters, nor does police training prepare officers to engage in a diagnostic process. In addition, proper and accurate psychiatric diagnosis requires many things officers often do not have with an individual in crisis: time, useful or complete background information, medical records, lab results, etc.

Another concern is the expectation many have related to what the line officer is actually able to do in a street encounter with a subject in crisis. The expectation often involves a belief officers can quickly recognize mental health conditions and do so with relative clarity and certainty. There has been a recent push in law enforcement to increase officer training related to psychiatric disorders, with the belief that by doing so, officers can be better prepared to address the crisis situations they encounter. This belief is inaccurate and creates an expectation of officers that is unrealistic, misleading, and potentially dangerous for the officer. It also conveys false information to the public, who are led to believe that officers can accurately diagnose on the street and should regularly do so. This poses not only a potential physical danger, but also a danger to the officer's career due to civil suits and various forms of disciplinary actions. While increasing officer education related to psychiatric diagnosis may have some value in furthering their understanding of the existence of these conditions, the level of suffering individuals experience related to these illnesses, and the consideration of alternatives to detention, it does not inherently prepare the officer to address the crisis situations that may arise.

I have also become concerned with having officers use clinical jargon and diagnostic classification related to potential civil liability. Officers are trained to use various diagnostic labels such as schizophrenia, depression, or bipolar disorder and jargon such as delusions, hallucinations, etc. These labels and jargon may then be noted in incident reports as explanations by the officer related to decision-making for intervention. Now, imagine an officer is involved with a person with mental illness and this incident leads to a force response in which the individual is injured or killed. The officer will likely be sued, and the first thing the plaintiff's attorney will do is jump on the clinical terms and jargon used by the officer. The questioning on the stand will go something like this:

> Attorney: "Officer Smith, you wrote in the incident report you believed this person had schizophrenia and that his delusions might lead him to harm his family, so you decided to intervene quickly with force."
>
> Officer Smith: "Yes, sir, that is correct."
>
> Attorney: "Officer, are you a psychologist?"
>
> Officer Smith: "No, sir."
>
> Attorney: "Do you have advanced clinical training that prepares you to diagnose someone?"

Well, you can clearly see where this goes. So, in essence, the concern is that in providing this type of training to officers, we are essentially setting them up to not only do things that even a psychologist can't do, which is diagnose on the street, but also to walk down a path that will potentially open them up to civil litigation. Now, imagine that same scenario where the officer describes what he sees using a thought-emotion-behavior observation as a means of decision-making. It doesn't require fancy academic training, and you don't need to be a psychologist to do it. It is a simple analysis of the basic elements of human functioning that can guide intervention strategies.

While mental health labeling has its place, for the officer on the street completing a specific police objective, it doesn't offer the best foundation for understanding what

6 | THE TEB MODEL

the officer is dealing with and how best to communicate. After the crisis has remitted and the officer is perhaps making decisions about placement or treatment, or for officers whose sole responsibility is working exclusively with persons with mental illness, advanced knowledge of diagnostic labels may make sense and can perhaps be quite useful. My focus is not to dismiss the value of diagnostic labels in certain contexts, but rather to convey that in the midst of a crisis, it should not be our primary focus in deciding how to immediately reduce crisis intensity. In fact, this book considers possible diagnostic considerations within each TEB profile for long-term planning and intervention.

WHAT THE TEB IS

Addressing the needs of a person in crisis, or what is often termed "de-escalation," requires focused education, training, and applied practice. Numerous programs related to communication, crisis intervention training, and de-escalation have been developed and are widely being offered around the country. The TEB was developed to address the important assessment piece within this type of training. The rationale behind its development is that when officers better understand the basic foundational human elements of the person they are interacting with, it prepares them to make better decisions as to how best to communicate, influence, and utilize persuasion with that person.

TEB provides a framework for quick analysis of a subject to determine not only if this person is in crisis, but also to determine if the person is not. While this may seem elementary on the surface, the swing toward de-escalation has created a troubling practice in law enforcement recently where officers are asked to de-escalate everything.

Again, a one-size-fits-all approach, which could potentially put the officer in jeopardy. Individuals in a crisis state require a specific form of communication and intervention, while someone who is not in crisis requires a different form of communication and intervention. Implementing the wrong intervention with the wrong person could certainly be problematic.

The TEB is a rapid assessment measure designed to direct line officers' attention to key functional elements (thought, emotion, and behavior) of a human being. This awareness provides important data the officer can then use in deciding the best way to approach an individual, the best form of communication for influencing the individual, and the most beneficial ways to move forward in achieving their specific police objective. The TEB:

- provides rapid assessment of a crisis situation
- informs officer understanding of a subject
- informs officer decision-making about intervention
- informs officer expectations about subject response
- informs officer explanation in report writing

WHAT THE TEB IS NOT

While the TEB can be useful in a variety of ways, there are also limitations. The TEB is not:

- a psychological test or diagnostic system
- a comprehensive program of crisis intervention or de-escalation
- able to predict future behavior
- something that should be memorized and/or used in a rote fashion without practice and training

- a justification to move directly to a force response due to a belief de-escalation would not be successful

WHAT IS A CRISIS?

The TEB profiles provide a simple, straightforward, and rapid means of assessing a person and offering an aid in forming decisions about how best to address a specific situation. The foundation of the formulation of this model involves not only a focus on the fundamental elements of human functioning, but also an operational definition of what constitutes a crisis.

While there are differing opinions on the definition of a crisis situation, the TEB model relies upon the fundamental theory that when a person has become unable to effectively and functionally cope with the demands of their environment and is unable to overcome what are perceived as unsurmountable obstacles, this constitutes a crisis situation. These types of situations are typically characterized by high emotion, low rationality, and an inability to cope with a serious problem perceived to be a serious threat (Vecchi, Van Hasselt, and Romano, 2005). While this could be a real conflict in one's environment, it can also result from hallucinations, delusions, or other significant distortions in thought that lead the individual to believe they are in danger or are facing a threat, even if this is not grounded in reality.

The term "mental health crisis" is also often used in law enforcement training. The meaning of this term, however, is unclear. The assumption is that an individual in crisis must be suffering from a mental illness. In reality, many who are in a crisis state are not mentally ill, nor have they ever been diagnosed with a mental illness. A crisis can be brought on by severe stressors in one's environment that can profoundly impact the individual's ability to cope. This can include a profound loss, traumatic exposure, etc. It can also result from a medical condition or exposure to a specific drug.

THE FLUIDITY OF TEB

An important element to consider related to the TEB profile is that it can change, and often does. While an officer may formulate an initial assessment of TEB, consistent observation and monitoring are critical. This is because TEB can change spontaneously, such as someone whose compliant behavior shifts suddenly and for no reason to noncompliance. The profile can also change in response to specific communication and intervention, with improvements being demonstrated. For example, a shift in someone demonstrating clear thought–high emotion–noncompliant behavior to clear thought–low emotion–compliant behavior. TEB profiles are not necessarily fixed and can quickly change for the worse or the better.

HOW TEB CAN BE USED

The TEB model has been used in a variety of ways by different officers and departments. Some use it as a training tool, integrating it into de-escalation education and high-fidelity training scenarios. Other departments have integrated it into policy, with a mandate to literally discuss the thought-emotion-behavior analysis within incident reports as a means of explaining officer decision-making related to intervention. This practice provides the scaffolding for officers to describe specifically what they saw which drove decision-making. Rather than a wandering narrative that incorporates poorly understood diagnostic labels or vague assumptions of mental illness, thought-emotion-behavior is specific and allows for clear communication about fundamental elements of functioning. Negotiators have used it in helping formulate an assessment of a subject as they develop ideas in how best to negotiate, when to stop negotiations, and the likelihood that negotiations will provide successful outcomes. Crisis intervention teams have used it for post-incident analysis in trying to better understand those who did not respond to crisis intervention strategies and ultimately required a force response for resolution. This type of analysis provides valuable data these teams can use in formulating decisions and developing strategies about how to best intervene in the future.

The TEB model was not designed, necessarily, to be memorized and carried around in a patrol car. Rather, it is a tool that can be used in training and education, reviewed, and analyzed for individual officers, and in some cases, if time provides, used as a formal guide for assessment and intervention.

THE SOAAR MODEL

The basic foundation of crisis intervention incorporates a process that includes the use of TEB. The SOARR model is a visual representation that explains the process of basic crisis intervention for an officer from the moment a call for service comes out through the successful resolution of the problem. In understanding this process, the use of TEB as an assessment tool is understood as a critical component to an overall assessment and intervention approach. The SOARR model is as follows:

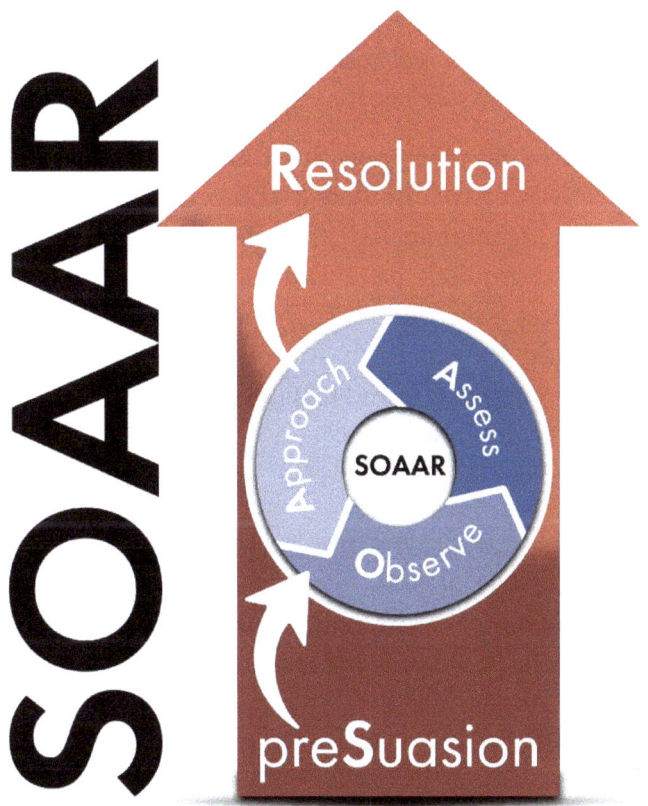

PreSuasion:

> The concept of preSuasion is that an officer can start the assessment of a subject and the subsequent thoughts related to communication and tactical planning when the dispatch call comes out and the officer is en route. For example, consider the following call:
>
> > *Respond to 123 Jones Avenue in response to a suspicious person. The complainant reports there is a man screaming outside of a*

store. He is not making any sense and appears very agitated. The store manager has tried to help him, but he will not listen.

Based simply upon this dispatch, an officer can already formulate a TEB profile. Specifically, contaminated thought–high emotion–noncompliant behavior. As such, while the officer is en route, with the assessment she has made, she can begin formulating ideas about communication and tactics before even seeing the individual.

Observe:

This relates to the officer's initial contact with a subject. Upon interaction, the officer is watching this individual and formulating a profile based on what she now actually sees.

Assess:

Based upon this observation, the officer then makes an assessment. Granted, she may have already made that assessment based on the dispatch call, but now she is either confirming it or changing her assessment based on what is now in front of her.

Approach:

Based on the assessment, the officer can now intervene with a specific approach. This could be a decision to use crisis communication or directive communication. This is essentially the intervention itself.

Ideally, the intervention would produce the desired effect and the officer would have a successful resolution of the crisis. In other words, a successful completion of the police objective. However, that is not always the case. As such, as the model reflects, the officer will now engage in a circular process of continually and fluidly observing, assessing, and approaching. This could involve another round or multiple rounds. This could take five minutes or several hours, depending on who and what the officer is dealing with. The above-mentioned idea that TEB is fluid is clearly illustrated by this circular element of the SOARR diagram, indicating that in crisis intervention, an officer is constantly observing and assessing, thus potentially necessitating a change in approach if they haven't reached a successful resolution.

CHAPTER II

TEB MODEL CONTENT

The fundamental element of this model is a focus on observing and understanding the thought, emotion, and behavior (TEB) of an individual rather than thinking from a psychiatric diagnosis perspective in sizing up someone quickly and deciding how best to intervene. The instrument attempts to simplify TEB by directing officers to consider two components within each area and use that information to rapidly formulate an assessment. After these two components are considered within the TEB, the officer then has a clear TEB profile, which forms the foundation of the assessment.

THOUGHT

The instrument directs officers to consider whether a subject's thinking is "clear" or "contaminated." A clear-minded person is able to utilize logical and rational thought. They are oriented to reality, know clearly who they are, and understand what is happening around them. They are not influenced by disorientation, delusions, hallucinations, or other perceptual disturbances. They are able to consider options presented to them in a clear, logical, and reasonable fashion, thus utilizing proper judgment and decision-making. Contaminated thought is a condition of thinking in which a person has lost the ability (either temporarily or permanently) to clearly, logically, and/or rationally understand their environment. This may be influenced by a variety of things including mental illness, drug intoxication, dementia, brain tumors, developmental disabilities such as autism, extreme mood problems, or other factors.

Officers are typically trained to focus on behavior, and little consideration is ever given to a focus on thought. Ironically, one of the most frequent mistakes officers make is trying to use logical persuasion with someone who, because of contaminated thought, lacks the ability to understand, process, and/or comprehend what is being said. In doing so, they run the risk of escalating the person by using ineffective communication strategies. Recognizing that a subject may be experiencing contaminated thinking can also provide valuable insight to the officer in better understanding why perhaps a subject is not responding appropriately to commands or directives.

In my years of working in psychiatric and forensic hospitals, jails, and on the street as a police officer, I have been amazed at the highly variable ways in which contaminated thought can be expressed by individuals. It varies considerably from one individual to another. Individuals with the same "diagnostic" category can present in dramatically different ways. For example, one individual with contaminated thought may not know who they are, where they are, or what is happening around them. They may demonstrate complete disorganization of thought and impaired reality testing. In other words, an inability to perceive accurately and logically what is happening around them. On the other hand, a contaminated thinker may also be someone who knows who they are, where they are, and what is happening around them, but is experiencing a very specific delusion (a false belief that is strongly held despite clear evidence to the contrary). Another individual may appear organized in their thinking, but then struggle with debilitating and frightening auditory command hallucinations (hearing voices others do not that may give commands). Another individual may be completely overwhelmed by emotion, and as such, demonstrate extreme limitations in judgment and decision-making due to high levels of emotional arousal and the loss of logical thinking ability. Consider an individual who is in the face of an officer yelling and screaming and cannot seem to respond to any command or attempts at reasonable communication. In all of these situations, contamination of thought is present, but how it presents itself can be highly variable.

Suicidal Thinking as Contaminated Thought

One interesting clinical phenomenon revolves around the question of whether a "suicidal person," or more specifically, someone who is contemplating ending their life, would be demonstrating contaminated thinking. In other words, is suicidal thought inevitably a contaminated thought process? The answer to this question is a resounding maybe.

Inspector (RET) Chris Butler, CEO of Raptor Protection, is a brilliant police trainer and we have often collaborated on many training programs together. We have also engaged in several spirited debates on this specific question. In his opinion, the decision to end one's life can be a logical decision. For example, someone who has a debilitating illness and experiences severe and chronic pain may make the logical decision to end their life. In today's world, we are seeing an increasing number of people working in conjunction with their physician to end their life due to a chronic and severe medical illness. An individual who has lost a spouse of fifty years may come to the conclusion that they can no longer live without the spouse and subsequently make a reasoned decision to end their life. Arguably, there are situations and circumstances where the thought process involved with ending one's life is a logical and rational one.

For the purposes of this model, however, the issue of suicidal thought is considered a contaminated thought process. The logic behind this decision is that for an individual who has come into contact with law enforcement related to suicidal thinking, it typically does not involve a logical thought process, but rather an impulsive, emotionally driven situation. These individuals are likely struggling with the decision and are engaged in an emotional back-and-forth. In addition, there is also a high probability they are under the influence of alcohol and/or drugs at the time, which has led to a desire to now act on something they have likely thought about in the past. The reduced control that accompanies substances is often the catalyst that turns thought into action.

If the suicidal thought process of a person is logical and rational, police officers are likely to not be involved, or when officers arrive, the subject has already committed the action. In the situation where suicidality reflects contamination of thought, the process is delayed and the subject is wrestling with the decision to take that final action.

EMOTION

The instrument directs officers to consider whether emotion is "high" or "low." While ideally, assessing emotion more in depth has value for various psychological assessments and interventions, in rapid assessment with subject encounters on the street, this does not appear necessary. Decisions related to a short-term assessment of emotion can be made based simply upon whether the subject an officer is interacting with is showing high levels of emotion or little emotion.

Emotion and thought share an intimate relationship. Each can affect the other. I can have thoughts that drive the intensity of my emotions. For example, I believe you have done something wrong to me, and in response, I feel strong anger. I may think I am a failure and that nothing I do will make any difference, thus driving high levels of sadness and hopelessness. High emotion can then impact thought. I may be experiencing very high levels of emotion, which then directly impacts my judgment and decision-making. My ability to reason logically can be impacted by high emotion. Thus the adage "don't make any serious decisions when emotional."

Emotion can also greatly impact behavior. If I am angry, I may be more argumentative, resistant, and less compliant. If I am sad, I may be withdrawn, isolate myself from others, or be limited in my interaction and movement.

As will be discussed later in this book, our awareness of a subject's emotions becomes critical in regard to our communication strategies. For example, if you are showing high levels of anger about something, I am going to acknowledge that anger and recognize it with you as a tactic to reduce it. So, some might look at the labeling of emotion in the model as just high or low and think, "There should be more to it than just high or low." Yes, the specific emotion you are showing certainly is relevant and valuable to know as I begin to intervene in addressing the crisis situation. However, for the purpose of rapid assessment, simply recognizing if the emotion is high or low gives me what I need to then formulate thoughts about how to deal with it. So, for assessment purposes, we focus on the level of the emotion as a first step.

BEHAVIOR

The instrument directs officers to consider whether behavior is "compliant" or "noncompliant." The concept of compliance revolves around an individual's willingness to engage and/or to follow the officer's suggestions or commands. It becomes especially important related to quick assessment. For instance, a subject's behavior may be disorganized or disruptive, but are they compliant with requests or directives? Many with problematic behaviors will still demonstrate compliance, while others will not. The level of compliance present in a subject helps inform our decision-making as to what we can do and what we cannot. It also is an important part of the overall initial assessment. Certainly, someone who is compliant is typically going to be easier to manage than someone who is not. That may not always be the case, but it is one less barrier we have to consider and cross in our attempts to address the crisis.

Another important consideration is that compliance versus noncompliance provides us with a lot of important data when we put it in the context of thought and emotion. For example, if someone is showing high emotion and noncompliance, we can safely assume the emotion is driving the noncompliance. That makes logical sense. If someone shows contaminated thought and they are noncompliant, we can assume the noncompliance is driven by the contaminated thought. For example, a person may be hearing voices telling them frightening things that distract them, which then leads them to fail to respond to your commands. Again, that makes logical sense. But, what about a person who is clear-minded, has low emotion, and is still noncompliant? That tells us a whole other story, and we realize then, this is more than just a crisis situation. This is someone who, despite the ability to think logically, persists in being noncompliant. It suggests to us their noncompliance is purposeful and is driven by something else.

THE TEB MODEL v5

Thought	Emotion	Behavior	Approach Style	Psychological Status	Volatility Risk	Volatility Type	Other Behavioral Factors to Consider
Contaminated	High	Compliant	Crisis comm	Likely mental health or drug	Moderate risk but be alert	Primal	Behavior difficult to predict/Watch for quick changes to noncompliant
Contaminated	High	Noncompliant	Crisis comm	Likely mental health or drug	High risk	Primal	Noncompliant likely due to confusion/ Suicide by cop often shows this profile
Contaminated	Low	Compliant	Crisis comm	Likely mental health or drug	Low risk but be alert	Primal	Likely sad but not shown outwardly
Contaminated	Low	Noncompliant	Crisis comm	Likely mental health or drug	Moderate risk but be alert	Primal	Noncompliance likely due to confusion/ Any violence likely due to confusion
Clear	High	Compliant	Crisis comm to reduce emotion then problem-solving strategies	Likely a mood problem or angry	Moderate risk but be alert	Cognitive or primal	Watch for compliance to change quickly
Clear	High	Noncompliant	Crisis comm to reduce emotion then problem-solving strategies	Likely a mood problem or angry	High risk	Cognitive or primal	High emotion driving noncompliance
Clear	Low	Compliant	Task-focused communication	Likely not mentally ill	Low risk but be alert	Cognitive	Potential compliant citizen/Watch for overcompliance as a pre-aggression cue
Clear	Low	Noncompliant	Directive comm (clarify limits and make aware of consequences)	Defiant/likely not mentally ill. Purposeful behavior	High risk	Cognitive	Noncompliance is purposeful/ Often anti-police/ Likely criminal minded and antisocial

THE TEB PROFILES

In considering a subject's presentation through a focus on thought, emotion, and behavior, we are then able to establish a clear TEB profile. It is from this profile we can then garner increased information about functioning and make some initial decisions about how to intervene. While it is impossible to predict the behavior of others, it is possible to recognize that various patterns of TEB do provide valuable information that helps inform our decisions and provides a foundation for how to intervene in achieving our police objective. It provides a scaffolding for what is important to pay attention to and when.

Each profile provides valuable information regarding a variety of factors for the officer to consider. While certainly not diagnostic in nature, it allows for a more complete understanding of the presentation so that an officer can not only make decisions about how best to intervene, but also provides insight into areas related to tactical considerations, possible etiology of the presentation, volatility potential, and other factors that might be relevant.

Within each profile, there are five specific areas of information that exist in addition to the profile itself. Each area provides information that aids in informing our awareness of the subject and providing useful information we can consider as we formulate tactics and communication strategies.

APPROACH STYLE

The approach style directs the officer toward the best form of communication and intervention. This is often an area where officers may struggle in deciding how to communicate with an individual. Diagnostic labels fall short in allowing for a basic understanding of what the officer is seeing and a strategy for intervention. However, a focus on basic elements of any mental illness such as thought, emotion, and behavior allows the officer critical information to then formulate an intervention strategy. It also allows for an avoidance of common mistakes officers often make, such as attempting to use logical persuasion with someone who is incapable of using that information successfully because they are illogical and unable to reason. For example, consider a subject who is cognitively disorganized and cannot think clearly. This will dramatically impact their capacity to not only listen to an officer's suggestions, but also their ability to process information in an organized fashion. In essence, the officer's words themselves become contaminated upon entering the subject's mind. What makes sense to the officer may not make sense to the subject. It is akin to trying to speak with someone who does not speak the same language. It doesn't matter how many times you say it, how loudly you say it, or in what manner you say it, they don't understand the language you are speaking.

A common issue related to approach style and contaminated thought is the officer's misunderstanding of why a subject may not be responding. Granted, there are some clear-minded people who simply ignore what officers say. However, I have seen many situations where a subject with contaminated thought doesn't respond the way the officer wants him to, which then leads the officer to perceive this as defiance or obstinance. This then upsets and escalates the officer, which subsequently upsets and escalates the subject. This is just one reason why proper approach style is critical, and if choosing the wrong one, we could inadvertently escalate the crisis.

The options considered within the approach style involve several key forms of communication designed specifically for the profile. There is some repetition across profiles, but also some dramatic differences depending on the presentation.

Crisis Communication

> Quite simply, crisis communication is communication designed to address a crisis situation. As obvious as this sounds, it may not be as clear as immediately suspected. Essentially, it suggests that rather than using direct commands, logical persuasion, or task-focused communication, the goal of the officer's communication will be to try to respond most appropriately to the individual's crisis state. It also takes into consideration the contamination that may be involved in a person's thinking that limits their ability to reason logically.
>
> In crisis communication, our primary focus is to listen. Rather than jumping in to solve a problem or give commands, we direct our communication strategy to the use of active listening to demonstrate empathy and eventually, hopefully, establish some form of influence over the person. As such, crisis communication involves an initial approach of listening, reframing what we hear to demonstrate we are listening, recognizing the emotional state of the individual, and demonstrating an empathetic presentation. We want the person in crisis to know we are listening,

we are invested in hearing what they have to say, and we are willing and prepared to offer support.

This form of communication is extremely powerful in helping someone with contaminated thinking feel safe and perhaps more organized, reducing emotional intensity and creating an environment designed to reduce the intensity of the crisis. While not a magic form of intervention and not a guarantee of success, it does increase the likelihood of reducing the crisis rather than escalating it.

In using this form of communication, our hope is that it reduces the crisis state of the subject. For example, perhaps lowering emotional intensity, increasing compliance, or allowing the contaminated thinker an easier time to engage. In the next step, when we reach a point in which our crisis communication has led to rapport and has reduced the intensity of the situation, we may be able to use problem-solving strategies with the individual to reach a resolution.

Example:

Sir, I can hear in your voice that you are frightened right now. You said that you are fearful because you believe someone has been poisoning your food and it has been making you sick?

Task-Focused Communication

Task-focused communication is the process of

conveying content to another individual. We are not invested in expressing emotion or venting about some issue, but rather in informing someone of key components and completing a task. For example, an officer may ask an individual for information necessary to complete an incident report. Or, the officer may gather information for someone during an accident in order to complete the accident report.

Example:

If you don't mind, I need to see a copy of your driver's license and insurance so I can complete the accident report. Also, I will need your phone number and address.

Directive Communication

Directive communication can be considered traditional police communication. Another way to say this would be to mention this is likely what you learned in the academy. Recall the concept of "first you ask, then you tell, and then you make." It allows for the conveyance of boundaries and expectations, as well as clear articulation of the consequence if someone does not comply. This form of communication is highly effective, and necessary, for some types of individuals.

Example:

I have asked you very clearly to step out of the vehicle to speak with me. You have failed to comply. Is there anything further I can do to gain your compliance? If not, I am going to be forced to remove you from the vehicle.

PSYCHOLOGICAL STATUS

In many situations, it is impossible for an officer, with the little information we often have available, to determine what may be causing a person's individual thought-emotion-behavior profile. In addition, knowing this may not be necessary for our initial task in trying to reduce a crisis situation. Certainly, if an officer has the time available to gather additional information, this can be helpful, but that is often not the case. In other situations, the person may not cooperate, making it challenging to completely understand what may be causing the situation.

In addressing psychological status within the model, the goal is to provide quick information to officers about what typically creates these types of profiles and the possible etiologies driving them. The model itself provides little complexity related to psychological status and instead offers some general information. Later in this book, we will explore further the possible mental health diagnoses that are linked to each type of thought-emotion-behavior presentation. This information could prove valuable for officers involved in more long-term planning for a person suffering from a mental illness.

VOLATILITY RISK

The volatility risk section provides a risk rating specific to the unpredictability of the subject based on the individual profile. This is not a risk prediction related to aggression, as this is impossible to do with limited information. Rather, it provides some insight into the level of unpredictability this individual may pose to officers and the likelihood of a strong, problematic reaction. This could potentially involve aggression, but also a strong emotional response as well.

VOLATILITY TYPE

Volatility and the unpredictable or impulsive reactions of subjects often have different objectives. For instance, an individual may react in an impulsive fashion based solely on an emotional response where perhaps the individual is overwhelmed with emotion and coping resources falter. This type of response is typically disorganized, nondirectional, and unplanned. Consider a subject with high emotion who is moving around a room in a disorganized fashion destroying items. This would be considered a primal response. On the other hand, a volitional response is purposeful, or what is termed instrumental. Consider the subject who calmly, thoughtfully attacks the officer. For the purpose of the model, the label used to describe this type of volatility is cognitive. It is an action with a purpose and is directed specifically toward the officer, perhaps as a means of avoiding arrest, harming the officer, or manipulating the officer in some fashion.

OTHER BEHAVIORAL FACTORS TO CONSIDER

Each individual TEB profile also provides other behavioral factors to consider based on clinical experience and empirical data. For example, the contaminated thought–high emotion–low compliance profile is typically associated with "suicide by cop," as most individuals in this situation demonstrate this type of profile. On the other hand, individuals with psychopathic traits or who would be considered "criminally minded" typically show a profile of clear thought–low emotion–noncompliant behavior. The goal of this specific section is to offer additional information to officers that might be useful in helping them make decisions about communication and tactics.

CHAPTER III

ANALYSIS AND CLINICAL EXAMPLES

The TEB model contains eight specific profiles that illustrate different thought-emotion-behavior patterns officers may encounter. Each profile presents its own unique clinical manifestation and subsequent challenges to address.

CONTAMINATED THOUGHT– HIGH EMOTION–COMPLIANT BEHAVIOR

Thought	Emotion	Behavior	Approach Style	Psychological Status	Volatility Risk	Volatility Type	Other Behavioral Factors to Consider
Contaminated	High	Compliant	Crisis comm	Likely mental health or drug	Moderate risk but be alert	Primal	Behavior difficult to predict/Watch for quick changes to noncompliant

This individual demonstrates clearly contaminated thinking as evidenced by a loss of logical thought. This can appear as someone who is actively having some type of hallucination, delusion, or disorganization in their ability to think clearly and logically. This is combined with a high level of emotion. Their behavior is compliant in that they demonstrate an ability and/or willingness to work with the officer in communication and/or the following of officer instructions.

This individual is typically confused, disoriented, and/or disorganized in their thinking. It could also manifest as organized thought, but a focused or specific hallucination or delusion. The contamination of their thinking will be fairly obvious in the clear lack of logical or reasonable thinking this individual is demonstrating. The high emotion is often driven by the contaminated thought. While not always, the emotional reactivity may be a response to the contamination of the thoughts, which drives the emotional state. Typically, this will be anger, anxiety, or fear, but can also manifest as sadness and/or frustration. This type of person is typically easy to interact with in that they are compliant and are motivated to convey their concerns to you. They are typically not confrontational, and the primary challenge revolves around their high emotion and contaminated thought processes.

Clinical Example:

Mr. Jones is a thirty-five-year-old male. As officers approach him, Mr. Jones mentions being fearful because he is being followed by drones programmed by the FBI. When questioned further, Mr. Jones proceeds to talk about the numerous drones he believes are spying on him throughout the day that are able to read his thoughts. He also expressed his concern that his thoughts are then being broadcast to others. He provided an example of the previous evening when he was watching the news, and they were talking about his thoughts. He is noticeably afraid and demonstrates this fear through physical nervousness in which he is shaking, sweating, and speaking quickly. As officers speak to him, he is cooperative and actively engaged in conversation with the officers and spontaneously expressing his concerns.

Approach Style:

The primary barriers for the officer to overcome in this individual profile are the contaminated thought of the individual and their high emotional state. Their compliance is a gift and something the officer should capitalize upon. For instance, reinforcing the compliance and conveying an appreciation of it to the individual. An example would be saying, "I appreciate your cooperation" or "I like that you are talking to me about this and want to encourage you to continue doing that."

The most beneficial strategy for communication for this protocol is crisis communication. This individual clearly is in a crisis state, and as such, will require communication and interaction focused on listening, reflecting, empathizing, and supporting. This should also involve communication that reflects on the emotional suffering of the person, identifying and recognizing their emotional state as a means of potentially reducing the intensity of the emotion. As such, the communication serves to recognize and acknowledge what the person may be thinking without agreeing with it, while also recognizing their emotional distress. Several key concepts to think about related to approach style are as follows:

- Stay calm and non-threatening in your demeanor.
- Speak in a gentle, reassuring tone.
- Avoid challenging or directly contradicting their beliefs or delusions. Instead, focus on validating

their emotions (e.g. "That sounds really distressing. I'm here to help you feel safe.").

- If they express delusional thoughts, gently redirect the conversation to neutral or comforting topics instead of debating their reality.

- Demonstrate patience and understanding, even if they struggle to articulate their thoughts or emotions.

- Guide, don't push. Offer suggestions rather than commands, as compliance can sometimes stem from fear or distress rather than true agreement. For instance: "Would you like to sit over here? It might feel more comfortable."

- Use clear, simple language to minimize confusion.

- Due to their high emotional state, help them regulate by creating a calm environment (lower noise, softer lighting, etc.).

- Encourage slow, deep breaths or grounding techniques if appropriate.

- Even if the person is compliant, avoid exploiting their vulnerability. Manipulation can harm trust and may exacerbate their condition.

- Focus on building a relationship based on care and respect.

Psychological Status:

While this can be highly variable and impossible to say for certain, typically this profile is influenced by a formal mental illness or drug intoxication. The most specific mental health diagnostic labels associated with this profile would be:

1. Schizophrenia Spectrum Disorders
    - **Contaminated Thought**: Hallucinations, delusions, and disorganized thinking are hallmark features.
    - **High Emotion**: Emotional dysregulation can occur, though flat affect is also common.
    - **Compliant Behavior**: In some cases, individuals may exhibit passive or compliant behavior, especially if overwhelmed by symptoms.
2. Bipolar Disorder (Manic or Mixed Episodes)
    - **Contaminated Thought**: Delusions or hallucinations can occur during severe manic or depressive episodes.
    - **High Emotion**: Intense mood swings, including elevated or irritable moods during mania.
    - **Compliant Behavior**: During depressive episodes, individuals may display compliant or passive behavior.
3. Borderline Personality Disorder (BPD)
    - **Contaminated Thought**: Brief psychotic-like episodes under stress.
    - **High Emotion**: Extreme emotional instability and intense interpersonal relationships.
    - **Compliant Behavior**: Fear of abandonment can lead to excessive compliance in some cases.

4. Delusional Disorder
   - **Contaminated Thought**: Presence of persistent delusions without other schizophrenia symptoms.
   - **High Emotion**: Emotional responses may align with the nature of the delusion.
   - **Compliant Behavior**: Often normal functioning except for the delusional beliefs.

5. Major Depressive Disorder with Psychotic Features
   - **Contaminated Thought**: Delusions or hallucinations typically congruent with depressive themes.
   - **High Emotion**: Intense sadness or despair.
   - **Compliant Behavior**: Passivity and compliance are common in severe depression.

6. Substance-Induced Psychotic Disorder
   - **Contaminated Thought**: Triggered by drug use or withdrawal.
   - **High Emotion**: Drug effects or withdrawal can lead to intense emotional states.
   - **Compliant Behavior**: May occur if influenced by situational factors or substance-induced dependency.

Volatility Risk:

The volatility risk for this profile is considered moderate but can change rather rapidly. The compliant nature of this individual's behavior serves as a protective factor in reducing overall volatility. Nonetheless, the elements of contaminated thought and high emotion drive forward the volatility risk.

Volatility Type:

While impossible to predict, typically the volatility of an individual with this profile is primal. The contaminated thought and high emotion often produce an emotionally reactive and disorganized pattern of behavior. This may also manifest as bizarre behaviors that are impulsively demonstrated, with little consideration of potential consequences for the actions.

Other Behavioral Factors to Consider:

The behavior of this individual can be difficult to predict and can change rapidly and with little provocation. Officers need to be very alert in interacting with this individual, especially in regard to the compliant presentation shifting rapidly and unpredictably to a noncompliant presentation.

CONTAMINATED THOUGHT– HIGH EMOTION–NONCOMPLIANT BEHAVIOR

Thought	Emotion	Behavior	Approach Style	Psychological Status	Volatility Risk	Volatility Type	Other Behavioral Factors to Consider
Contaminated	High	Noncompliant	Crisis comm	Likely mental health or drug	High risk	Primal	Noncompliant likely due to confusion/ Suicide by cop often shows this profile

This individual also demonstrates contaminated thinking as evidenced by a loss of logical thought. This can appear as someone who is actively having some type of hallucination, delusion, or disorganization in their ability to think clearly and logically. This is combined with a high level of emotion and is now complicated by noncompliant behavior, which makes management and influence of this individual far more complicated than with a compliant individual.

This individual is typically confused, disoriented, and/or disorganized in their thinking. However, there could also be the presence of some type of delusion or hallucination within the context of organized thought. The contamination of their thinking will be fairly obvious in the clear lack of logical or reasonable thinking this individual is demonstrating. While not always, the emotional reactivity may be a response to the contamination of the thoughts, which drives the emotional state. Typically, this will be anger, anxiety, or fear, but can also manifest as sadness and/or frustration. However, it is also possible that this individual has reached a point of emotional intensity in which their thinking has now become contaminated. There are individuals whose thinking can deteriorate when experiencing high levels of emotion. These challenges become much more complex with the addition of noncompliant behavior, which dramatically increases the difficulty in influencing this individual.

Confusion is also a predominant characteristic that may, in part, drive the noncompliant elements of behavior. In other words, the individual may not understand or process what is being requested of him and, as such, respond with behaviors that are reflective of noncompliance.

Clinical Example:

Mr. Smith is a fifty-year-old male. Officers are called in response to a disturbance outside of a local grocery store. As an officer approaches Mr. Smith, he immediately begins to yell at the officer to get back and leave him alone. He says, "Somebody in that store has the detonator." The officer attempts to make sense of what is being said and

Mr. Smith again makes the statement related to a detonator and his plan to enter the store to search for customers to find the detonator. He says the detonator will cause the chip in his son's head to explode and he must stop it from happening. The officer attempts to redirect Mr. Smith, who proceeds to push by him and attempts to run into the store.

Approach Style:

Arguably, this is the most challenging profile to manage. Not only is there the contamination of thought and high emotion to address, but also now the addition of noncompliance. All three elements of functioning are impacted in a dysfunctional fashion, rendering the individual less likely to conform to or comply with officers' attempts at engagement.

The gift of compliance is typically the pathway we can travel to address thought contamination and high emotion. Without it, we are now battling on multiple fronts, and interacting with someone in this crisis state often feels hopeless and as if nothing we do will make much of a difference. The pushback we get from the individual, as manifest through noncompliance, is often intense in this profile and serves to cripple our attempts to address the contaminated thought and high emotion.

This individual is clearly in a crisis state. The most beneficial strategy for communication for this protocol is crisis communication. Once again, even though this individual is noncompliant, we must persist in our attempts to listen, reflect, empathize, and support. Unlike our first profile, where compliance may help garner a quick response, this individual may show no response to our attempts and may in fact respond with negativity and increased emotional intensity. Patience is certainly key in interacting with an individual in this crisis state. Several key concepts to think about related to approach style are as follows:

- Stay calm while maintaining a composed and non-threatening demeanor.
- Validate their emotions without reinforcing delusions ("I can see this feels very real to you.").
- Avoid confrontation in that challenging beliefs can increase distress or defensiveness.
- Show empathy through listening without interrupting or judging.
- Speak slowly and calmly to model composure.
- Reflect their emotions to show understanding ("I can see that you're feeling very angry right now.").
- If possible, provide both space and time. Sometimes stepping back can settle emotions.
- Focus on asking open-ended questions to help identify underlying concerns.
- Break down complex tasks into manageable steps.
- Make sure to praise behavior that involves any semblance of compliant behavior or response as a means of encouraging it to continue.
- Offer choices as a means of empowering their autonomy.

Psychological Status:

While this can be highly variable and impossible to say for certain, typically this profile is influenced by a formal mental illness or drug intoxication. The most specific diagnostic labels associated with this profile would be:

1. Schizophrenia Spectrum and Other Psychotic Disorders
   - **Contaminated Thought**: Hallucinations (e.g. hearing voices) and delusions (false, fixed beliefs).
   - **High Emotion**: Emotional dysregulation may occur during episodes of psychosis.
   - **Noncompliant Behavior**: May result from lack of insight into the illness (anosognosia).

2. Bipolar Disorder (with Psychotic Features)
   - **Contaminated Thought**: Can occur during manic or depressive episodes, involving delusions or hallucinations.
   - **High Emotion**: Intense mood swings ranging from mania (high energy, euphoria) to depression.
   - **Noncompliant Behavior**: May stem from feelings of invincibility during mania or hopelessness during depression.

3. Borderline Personality Disorder (BPD)
   - **Contaminated Thought**: Transient, stress-related psychotic symptoms (e.g. paranoia).
   - **High Emotion**: Intense emotional reactions and difficulty managing them.
   - **Noncompliant Behavior:** Often linked to interpersonal conflicts or mistrust.

4. Substance-Induced Psychotic Disorder
   - **Contaminated Thought**: Caused by drug use or withdrawal.
   - **High Emotion**: Substance use can amplify emotional instability.
   - **Noncompliant Behavior**: Defiance driven by psychoactive effects of the drug.
5. Post-Traumatic Stress Disorder (PTSD)
   - **Contaminated Thought**: Flashbacks or dissociation can sometimes mimic psychosis.
   - **High Emotion**: Heightened anxiety, anger, or fear triggered by trauma reminders.
   - **Noncompliant Behavior** Distrust in authority or difficulty engaging with others.

Volatility Risk:

The volatility risk for this profile is considered high. As mentioned, an individual with this profile can be unpredictable, with a strong potential for disruptive and problematic behaviors. This can include aggression, but that is not always the case. If aggression is present, it can often be spontaneous and without any nonverbal indicators. It also can be brought on quickly without any overt precipitating factors.

Volatility Type:

While noncompliance tends to increase volatility risk, it doesn't seem to change the type. Even in the face of noncompliance, volatility is primal in this profile and typically in response to confusion, cognitive disorganization, and/or high emotion. Reactions are typically impulsive and poorly thought through, with a strong emotional flavor. If someone like this were to physically attack, the attack would likely be poorly organized and spontaneous.

Other Behavioral Factors to Consider:

A critical finding in relation to this profile is that it is typically associated with "suicide by cop" situations. As previously discussed, the suicidal thought process is considered contaminated, with high emotion and noncompliance fueling the self-harm fire. In high-stress situations with suicidal subjects, high emotion and noncompliant behaviors are commonly witnessed. This finding was initially based on clinical observation and experience but has since been reinforced through data produced through police interaction and analysis. In their 2020 Crisis Intervention Team Annual Report, the San Francisco Police Department completed an after-incident analysis of TEB profiles related to cases identified as likely or definite "suicide by cop" situations. In their findings, 100 percent of these cases involved a profile of contaminated thought, high emotion, and noncompliant behavior.

An additional finding of relevance to this profile is the likelihood of de-escalation attempts being unsuccessful as well. When the San Francisco Crisis Intervention Team reviewed data in their 2020, 2021, 2022, and 2023 annual reports, they repeatedly found that in use-of-force situations with crisis subjects, a predominant number of cases fell within this profile. While it is never good practice to use this profile as a means of avoiding de-escalation, findings do suggest that in cases where force was used, the majority of the cases involved this specific profile, reflecting the difficulties in dealing with this specific combination of thought, emotion, and behavior. While it is critical that officers never neglect tactical awareness in lieu of de-escalation strategies, nowhere is this more important than when faced with someone demonstrating this challenging combination of thought, emotion, and behavior.

CONTAMINATED THOUGHT-LOW EMOTION-COMPLIANT BEHAVIOR

Thought	Emotion	Behavior	Approach Style	Psychological Status	Volatility Risk	Volatility Type	Other Behavioral Factors to Consider
Contaminated	Low	Compliant	Crisis comm	Likely mental health or drug	Low risk but be alert	Primal	Likely sad but not shown outwardly

In this profile, we are faced with an individual who, while demonstrating contaminated thought, also demonstrates low emotion and a compliant presentation. This individual is likely to present as rather bland and lackluster, with little outward expression of emotion and when they do comply with officer commands, it may be slow and rather lethargic. Any communication an officer receives from this type of individual will clearly reflect the contamination of their thinking as evidenced by discussion of hallucinations or the demonstration of some type of delusion. They also could appear cognitively disorganized and have no realistic grounding in reality. Yet, in the presence of these thought distortions and absence of logical thinking, they are rather emotionless and compliant in their interactions.

In considering all the combinations of profiles within individuals with contaminated thought, this profile is the easiest to work with. While challenged with the contaminated thinking, we are free from the intensity of emotion and the challenges of noncompliance.

Clinical Example:

Ms. Chavez is a fifty-five-year-old female. Officers are dispatched to her home after her husband called to express concerns about her. When officers arrive, they find her sitting in a chair staring blankly at the wall. In attempts to communicate with her, officers are quickly alerted to her disorganized thoughts as she begins to speak in unintelligible words that are tangential and random. She communicates freely, but little she talks about makes sense. She demonstrates little emotion. When officers ask if she would be willing to go to the hospital for evaluation, Ms. Chavez gets up from the chair and freely walks with officers to the ambulance.

Approach Style:

While there is no intensity of emotion and noncompliance to address, the contamination of thought in and of itself constitutes a crisis situation. Any time there is an absence of logical thought, this individual is going to be unable to reason through the demands of the environment in a successful fashion, thus constituting a crisis. While this profile may not represent the typical problematic behavior and emotion commonly seen in someone with high emotion and noncompliant behavior, we are still faced with the lack of logical reasoning ability that an individual depends upon daily to make rational decisions and utilize effective judgment.

Because this profile still constitutes a crisis situation, the most beneficial strategy for communication is crisis communication. Several key concepts to think about related to approach style are as follows:

- Individuals with contaminated thought may experience delusions, hallucinations, or distorted thinking. It's essential to avoid challenging their perceptions directly, as it could lead to defensiveness and potentially increase emotionality and/or turn compliance into noncompliance.
- This individual may demonstrate limited emotional expression and a lack of emotional response, which doesn't mean they don't care, but rather may be struggling to express feelings.
- Their compliant behavior may stem from vulnerability, fear, or a desire to avoid conflict.
- Be consistent, honest, and patient in your interactions.
- Listen actively and validate their feelings without dismissing their experiences.
- Avoid judgment or expressing disbelief about their perceptions.
- Use simple, clear, and concise language.
- Avoid sarcasm, humor that might be misinterpreted, or overly emotional expressions.
- Speak in a calm, supportive tone.

Psychological Status:

While this can be highly variable and impossible to say for certain, typically this profile is influenced by a formal mental illness or drug intoxication. The most specific diagnostic labels associated with this profile would be:

1. Schizophrenia (Negative Symptoms Prominent)
   - **Contaminated Thought**: Hallucinations, delusions, or disorganized thinking.
   - **Low Emotion**: Flat affect, reduced emotional expressiveness.
   - **Compliant Behavior:** Often passive due to lack of motivation (avolition) or social withdrawal.
2. Schizoaffective Disorder
   - **Contaminated Thought**: Hallucinations, delusions, or disorganized thinking.
   - **Low Emotion**: This can include depression and/or limited emotional responses, as well as negative symptoms like low emotional expression.
   - **Compliant Behavior**: Compliant/passive behavior can also be present.
3. Delusional Disorder (Subtypes)
   - **Contaminated Thought**: Focused delusions without broader disorganization.
   - **Low Emotion**: Low emotion can develop in chronic cases.
   - **Compliant Behavior**: Compliance may develop, especially in chronic cases.
4. Depressive Disorders with Psychotic Features
   - **Contaminated Thought**: May occur, particularly delusions or hallucinations tied to depressive themes.
   - **Low Emotion**: Profound sadness, flat affect.
   - **Compliant Behavior**: Often due to feelings of worthlessness or hopelessness.

5. Catatonia (Associated with Several Disorders)
   - **Contaminated Thought**: Present in underlying conditions like schizophrenia or mood disorders.
   - **Low Emotion**: Minimal response or emotional display.
   - **Compliant Behavior**: Extreme suggestibility in catatonic states.
6. Autism Spectrum Disorder (ASD) with Psychosis
   - **Contaminated Thought**: Some individuals with ASD may develop psychotic symptoms in adulthood.
   - **Low Emotion**: Reduced affect might overlap with ASD traits.
   - **Compliant Behavior**: May result from social naivety or a tendency to follow routines and rules.
7. Dementia or Neurocognitive Disorders
   - **Contaminated Thought**: Delusions or hallucinations may occur in later stages.
   - **Low Emotion**: Flat affect due to neurodegeneration.
   - **Compliant Behavior**: A passive demeanor due to cognitive decline.

Volatility Risk:

The volatility risk for this profile is considered low, but it is important to remain alert. While it is easy to believe someone with this profile would be passive due to their compliance and low emotionality, this could shift rapidly into more volatile behaviors. A basic rule of thumb is that anyone with contaminated thought can be volatile and unpredictable. This is typically related to the absence of logic and reasoning ability, which is key to making solid decisions and controlling behavior.

Volatility Type:

If this individual were to become volatile, the likely demonstration of this volatility would be primal in nature. Even though there is no emotion driving a volatile reaction, their behavior can often turn volatile within the context of a calm demeanor. While absent of emotion for fuel, the volatile behavior would still likely not be organized, purposeful, or goal-directed. This would appear as an impulsive "flailing around" in a disorganized fashion.

Other Behavioral Factors to Consider:

Individuals demonstrating this protocol are often sad and dysphoric, with little energy and a rather apathetic demeanor. However, as mentioned, they are not likely to demonstrate emotion in any direct fashion, and their overall demeanor will be flat and nonresponsive.

CONTAMINATED THOUGHT–
LOW EMOTION–NONCOMPLIANT BEHAVIOR

Thought	Emotion	Behavior	Approach Style	Psychological Status	Volatility Risk	Volatility Type	Other Behavioral Factors to Consider
Contaminated	Low	Noncompliant	Crisis comm	Likely mental health or drug	Moderate risk but be alert	Primal	Noncompliance likely due to confusion / Any violence likely due to confusion

The individual with this profile will have similarities to our previous profile as related to contaminated thought and low emotion. However, what complicates this profile is the noncompliant behavioral presentation. As such, our two specific challenges here revolve around the contamination of thought and the individual's refusal to comply with attempts at interaction. Typically, this noncompliance will be a result of confusion and/or disorientation rather than high emotion. In this profile, it is typically the contamination itself that drives the noncompliance.

Clinical Example:

Mr. Sullen is a twenty-five-year-old male. He is spotted wandering aimlessly around a warehouse parking lot. He is talking to himself. As officers attempt to make contact with him, he moves away from them and will not engage them in any manner. His statements to himself are highly disorganized and make little sense to the officers. As they attempt to communicate with Mr. Sullen, he persistently walks away and continues talking to himself.

Approach Style:

Based on our understanding of a crisis situation, Mr. Sullen is in a crisis state. He lacks the logical reasoning ability to make proper decisions and his behavior is random and chaotic. He appears emotionless, but his thinking distortion and noncompliance are evident. In response to a profile such as this, the most appropriate form of intervention is through the use of crisis communication. Several key concepts to think about related to approach style are as follows:

- Consider speaking in a calm, clear voice. Avoid confrontation or argument about any statements made reflecting contaminated thinking.
- Use clear, simple sentences to avoid confusion.
- Allow time for them to process and respond, as they may take longer to engage.

- Reassure the individual you are there to support them.
- While not moving to close the space between you and the subject, do provide some parameters or boundaries to ensure the individual's safety.
- Work to ensure the environment is free from triggers that might intensify their distress.
- Try to demonstrate an understanding of their situation, even if they don't reciprocate verbally or visually.
- Understand their noncompliance likely stems from confusion, mistrust, or a lack of insight into their condition.
- Avoid forcing compliance, but explain the benefits and offer choices to give them a sense of control.

Psychological Status:

While this can be highly variable and impossible to say for certain, typically this profile is influenced by a formal mental illness or drug intoxication. The most specific diagnostic labels associated with this profile would be:

1. Schizophrenia

- **Contaminated Thought**: Hallucinations, delusions, and disorganized thinking.
- **Low Emotion**: Flat affect, reduced emotional expression, and social withdrawal.
- **Noncompliant Behavior**: Difficulty adhering to treatment or societal expectations, sometimes due to lack of insight (anosognosia).

2. Schizoaffective Disorder
   - **Contaminated Thought**: Similar psychotic symptoms to schizophrenia.
   - **Low Emotion**: Emotional blunting or incongruence may be present during psychotic episodes.
   - **Noncompliant Behavior**: Noncompliance may occur due to mood fluctuations or psychotic experiences.
3. Schizotypal Personality Disorder
   - **Contaminated Thought**: Paranoid ideation or odd beliefs.
   - **Low Emotion**: Constricted range of emotional expression and awkward social interactions.
   - **Noncompliant Behavior**: Eccentric behaviors and resistance to social norms.
4. Major Depressive Disorder with Psychotic Features
   - **Contaminated Thought**: Delusions or hallucinations related to depressive themes.
   - **Low Emotion**: Depressed mood, diminished interest in activities, and low emotional reactivity.
   - **Noncompliant Behavior**: Resistance to interaction due to despair or cognitive distortions.
5. Bipolar Disorder with Psychotic Features
   - **Contaminated Thought**: May occur during manic or depressive episodes.
   - **Low Emotion**: Emotional flattening, especially in depressive phases.
   - **Noncompliant Behavior**: Impulsivity or refusal to follow advice, especially during depressive episodes.

6. Autism Spectrum Disorder (ASD) with Psychosis

- **Contaminated Thought**: Some individuals with ASD may develop psychotic symptoms in adolescence or adulthood.
- **Low Emotion**: Emotional expression may be restricted or atypical in ASD.
- **Noncompliant Behavior**: Noncompliance may stem from rigidity or difficulty understanding social expectations.

7. Substance-Induced Psychotic Disorder

- **Contaminated Thought**: Triggered by substance use or withdrawal (e.g. hallucinations or paranoia).
- **Low Emotion**: Emotional numbing due to substance effects or long-term use.
- **Noncompliant Behavior**: Risky behaviors, refusal to seek help, or substance use despite consequences.

8. Delusional Disorder

- **Contaminated Thought**: Fixed delusions without broader disorganization of thought.
- **Low Emotion**: Constricted affect in nondelusional interactions.
- **Noncompliant Behavior**: Refusal to accept evidence that contradicts delusions.

Volatility Risk:

The volatility risk for this profile is considered moderate. This risk rating is due to the combination of contaminated thought and noncompliance, which tend to drive up the risk a bit. While likely not as volatile as individuals demonstrating contaminated thought, high emotion, and noncompliance, officers should be alert to quick changes from moderate to high risk. The risk would certainly escalate should the individual begin to show increases in negative emotion. In addition, the disorganized and confused thinking of this individual that drives the noncompliance can quickly escalate, thus raising risk as well.

Volatility Type:

If this individual were to become volatile, the likely demonstration of this volatility would be primal in nature. Even though there is no emotion driving a volatile reaction, their behavior can often turn volatile within the context of a calm demeanor. While absent of emotion for fuel, the volatile behavior would still likely not be organized, purposeful, or goal-directed. Any volatile reaction would likely be driven by disorganized thought processes.

Other Behavioral Factors to Consider:

As mentioned, the noncompliance of an individual demonstrating this profile would likely be a result of disorganized thought and confusion. Any resistance is likely not going to be an intentional attempt to manipulate, deceive, or otherwise provoke. Rather, it will quickly become apparent to officers that the noncompliance of the individual is generated by the dysfunction of their thought processes.

CLEAR THOUGHT–
HIGH EMOTION–COMPLIANT BEHAVIOR

Thought	Emotion	Behavior	Approach Style	Psychological Status	Volatility Risk	Volatility Type	Other Behavioral Factors to Consider
Clear	High	Compliant	Crisis comm to reduce emotion then problem-solving strategies	Likely a mood problem or angry	Moderate risk but be alert	Cognitive or primal	Watch for compliance to change quickly

An individual demonstrating this profile demonstrates the ability to think logically and rationally despite the presence of high emotion. There are individuals who experience high emotion but whose thinking is not contaminated specifically by the presence of this emotion. In this profile, while emotion is high, the individual remains compliant with officer commands and/or interactions. The primary challenge with this profile is the presence of high emotion, yet we have the gift of logical reasoning ability and a compliant form of interaction.

Clinical Example:

Ms. Rodriguez is a thirty-three-year-old female who has been stopped by police for running a stop sign. As the officer approaches the vehicle, Ms. Rodriguez immediately begins yelling at the officer and arguing about the legitimacy of the stop. Her arguments are reasonable, nonbizarre, and appropriately organized. She is very angry and argues the officer has been following her and has purposefully targeted her because of her race. As the officer requests various documents subsequent to the stop, Ms. Rodriguez provides the information as requested. She also answers the officer's questions, albeit while yelling in an angry manner.

Approach Style:

Individuals in this situation are experiencing a crisis due to the intensity of the emotion. Any time there is the presence of high emotion in an individual related to police interaction, it is more appropriate to address it as a crisis situation due to the potential volatility that can occur and the potential for the situation to deteriorate rapidly. High emotion is a pathway to deterioration in both thought and compliance level, and as such, it must be addressed carefully. In this type of profile, our primary goal of communication is in attempting to bring down the intensity of the emotion and then implementing problem-solving strategies. Several key concepts to think about related to approach style are as follows:

- Validate the individual's feelings to show understanding and build rapport, even if you disagree with what they say is driving the emotion.
- Avoid dismissing or minimizing their emotions, even if their behavior is compliant.
- Use a calm, steady tone of voice.
- Maintain open body language to signal approachability and respect.
- Encourage the individual to share more about their thoughts and feelings.
- Let them express their emotions and thoughts without interruption. Avoid the temptation to argue or engage them in a power struggle.
- Use active listening by summarizing or paraphrasing what they say.
- Leverage their clear thinking to engage in productive problem-solving.

- Ask open-ended questions to encourage critical thinking or solutions.
- Acknowledge the emotion while gently steering the conversation toward rational outcomes.
- Recognize and reinforce their willingness to engage and cooperate.

Psychological Status:

Individuals with this profile may simply be experiencing a strong emotional reaction to a specific situation and have no specific history of mental health concerns. However, there are a number of different diagnostic classifications that might also lead to this type of profile. The most specific diagnostic labels associated with this profile would be:

1. Generalized Anxiety Disorder (GAD)

- **Clear Thought**: Individuals often overthink and strive to maintain control. Thinking is logical and often hyper-logical.
- **High Emotion**: Heightened emotional state brought on by strong feelings of anxiety.
- **Compliant Behavior**: Will often demonstrate compliant behavior to avoid conflict or perceived threats.

2. Social Anxiety Disorder

- **Clear Thought**: These individuals are typically logical in thought.
- **High Emotion**: A fear of negative judgment can result in emotional reactivity.

- **Compliant Behavior**: The fear of negative judgment may also result in compliant behavior.

3. Obsessive-Compulsive Personality Disorder (OCPD)
   - **Clear Thought**: These individuals will often exhibit clear and detailed thought patterns.
   - **High Emotion**: Intense emotional responses can occur when things deviate from expectations.
   - **Compliant Behavior**: Behavior is compliant with rules or authority figures.

4. Dependent Personality Disorder
   - **Clear Thought**: Cognitive clarity is preserved in striving to maintain relationships.
   - **High Emotion**: Intense emotional responses are influenced by a strong need for care and approval from others.
   - **Compliant Behavior**: The same strong need for care and approval that drives high emotion can also lead to compliant behavior.

5. Emotionally Intense Conditions (e.g. High-Functioning Autism)
   - **Clear Thought**: Thought processes in these individuals typically remain clear and logical.
   - **High Emotion**: Some of these individuals can have heightened emotional responses.
   - **Compliant Behavior**: They often may engage in compliant behavior to fit social norms.

Volatility Risk:

The volatility risk for this profile is considered moderate. This risk rating is due to the presentation of high emotion. While clear thinking and compliant behavior certainly are considered preventative factors in reducing volatility, the mere presence of elevated emotion does increase the risk.

Volatility Type:

The volatility type for this profile is mixed and could involve primal responses or more instrumental responses. In other words, any volatility in response to high emotion could be impulsive and driven by the intensity of the emotion, but could also be targeted behavior designed to harm, punish, or avoid an officer. The presence of logical thought allows for the cognitive organization needed for purposeful volatility.

Other Behavioral Factors to Consider:

Due to the presence of high emotion, the compliance rating of the individual could shift rapidly. Specifically, from compliant behavior to noncompliant behavior. This is due to the unpredictable nature of high emotion, especially if officer attempts to reduce emotional intensity prove to be futile.

CLEAR THOUGHT–HIGH EMOTION–NONCOMPLIANT BEHAVIOR

Thought	Emotion	Behavior	Approach Style	Psychological Status	Volatility Risk	Volatility Type	Other Behavioral Factors to Consider
Clear	High	Noncompliant	Crisis comm to reduce emotion then problem-solving strategies	Likely a mood problem or angry	High risk	Cognitive or primal	High emotion driving noncompliance

In this profile, we are dealing with a challenging combination of high emotion and noncompliant behavior. Fortunately, logical thinking is still intact. While this might initially seem to make things better, in reality, we have someone who, even while demonstrating a capacity for logical thought, remains noncompliant within the context of high emotion. The high emotion is likely driving the noncompliance and is going to be the primary area we need to target to bring the individual online as far as compliance is concerned.

Clinical Example:

Officers are called to a suspicious person. Upon arrival, they see an individual and begin to question him. He immediately yells at officers that they have no right to stop him and question him. He yells repeatedly that they are violating his rights. Officers request identification and he refuses to provide it. He begins to argue legal statute and repeatedly challenges the officers' authority to intervene with him.

Approach Style:

The intensity of the emotion is being displayed in a dysfunctional manner through noncompliant behavior. This individual is not coping effectively, as evidenced by noncompliance with law enforcement. In this type of profile, our primary goal of communication is in attempting to bring down the intensity of the emotion. As such, our communication will be directed toward crisis communication to bring down emotion and then initiate problem-solving strategies. Several key concepts to think about related to approach style are as follows:

- Communicate in a manner designed to let the individual know their feelings are understood.
- Avoid dismissing or minimizing the emotion, as this could escalate the situation.
- Remain composed, even if the person is highly emotional and/or disrespectful/rude to you.
- Model calmness in your demeanor.
- Attempt to leverage their clear thought by presenting your thoughts logically and concisely.
- Avoid overloading the individual with information. Focus specifically on essential facts.
- Find common ground by identifying shared goals or values to build rapport.
- Present options to give them a sense of control while steering toward a solution.
- Clarify limits and state boundaries without sounding punitive.
- Be firm, yet flexible. This allows room for compromise while standing firm with core principles.
- Redirect emotional outbursts or noncompliance toward the desired outcome.

Psychological Status:

Individuals with this profile may simply be experiencing a strong emotional reaction to a specific situation and have no specific history of mental health concerns. However, there are a number of different diagnostic classifications that might also lead to this type of profile. Typically, if a formal mental health condition is present, it is often a formal personality disorder. The most specific diagnostic labels associated with this profile would be:

1. Borderline Personality Disorder (BPD)

- **Clear Thought**: People with BPD may express logical reasoning when discussing their experiences, but their thoughts might be skewed by fear of abandonment or interpersonal conflict.
- **High Emotion**: Intense emotional reactions, including anger, sadness, or fear, are hallmark features.
- **Noncompliant Behavior**: Acting out or refusing to follow expectations often stems from perceived invalidation or emotional distress.

2. Narcissistic Personality Disorder (NPD)

- **Clear Thought**: Individuals with NPD often articulate their thoughts clearly, especially in areas where they feel competent or superior.
- **High Emotion**: They can display heightened emotional reactions when their self-esteem is threatened.
- **Noncompliant Behavior:** Noncompliance may manifest as defiance or refusal to follow rules that conflict with their perceived superiority.

3. Oppositional Defiant Disorder (ODD)

- **Logical Thought**: Children or adolescents with ODD may use logical reasoning to justify their defiance.
- **High Emotion**: Anger and frustration are frequent emotional states.
- **Noncompliant Behavior**: Persistent refusal to comply with authority figures or rules is a defining characteristic.

4. Autism Spectrum Disorder (ASD) with Co-Occurring Conditions

- **Clear Thought**: Logical or rigid thinking is common, often tied to their preference for routines or rules.
- **High Emotion**: Emotional dysregulation, including meltdowns or outbursts, may occur when routines are disrupted.
- **Noncompliant Behavior**: Noncompliance might stem from difficulty understanding social expectations or sensory overload.

5. Paranoid Personality Disorder (PPD)

- **Logical Thought**: Individuals may present their ideas in a coherent, logical manner, but their logic is often influenced by mistrust or suspicion.
- **High Emotion**: Strong emotional reactions, such as anger or fear, may arise from perceived threats or betrayals.
- **Noncompliant Behavior**: Noncompliance often results from distrust in authority figures or systems.

6. Antisocial Personality Disorder (APD)

- **Logical Thought**: Individuals are typically clear and coherent in their thinking, with the ability for logical reasoning.
- **High Emotion**: Strong emotional reactions occur, primarily anger and irritability.
- **Noncompliant Behavior**: This is a core symptom of the condition, with a pattern of defiance in response to authority and social norms.

Volatility Risk:

The volatility risk for this profile is considered high. The combination of high emotion and noncompliance drives the risk elevation.

Volatility Type:

The volatility type for this profile is mixed and could involve primal responses or more instrumental responses. In other words, any volatility in response to high emotion could be impulsive and driven by the intensity of the emotion, but could also be targeted behavior designed to harm, punish, or avoid an officer. The presence of logical thought allows for the cognitive organization needed for purposeful volatility.

Other Behavioral Factors to Consider:

In this profile, the high emotion is likely driving the noncompliant behavior. The hope is that with a reduction in emotional intensity, compliance will shift from noncompliant to compliant. This is not a certainty, but oftentimes when emotional intensity is reduced, a person becomes more compliant.

CLEAR THOUGHT-LOW EMOTION-COMPLIANT BEHAVIOR

Thought	Emotion	Behavior	Approach Style	Psychological Status	Volatility Risk	Volatility Type	Other Behavioral Factors to Consider
Clear	Low	Compliant	Task-focused communication	Likely not mentally ill	Low risk but be alert	Cognitive	Potential compliant citizen/Watch for overcompliance as a pre-aggression cue

This profile involves a thought-emotion-behavior combination that would be typical of a rational, emotionally balanced, compliant citizen. That is the most likely scenario of this presentation. However, it must be stated that an individual with the intention to harm an officer could also falsely present this pattern as a means of psychological manipulation. In other words, a ruse to make the officer let down his guard and reduce tactical awareness. The specific goal would be to have the officer perceive the individual as nonthreatening and as a low risk.

In specific research conducted by the Federal Bureau of Investigation assessing felonious assaults on law enforcement (Pinizzotto and Davis, 1992; Pinizzotto, Davis, and Miller, 1997; Pinizzotto, Davis, and Miller, 2006), data indicates that many of the officers killed in the line of duty "perceived cooperation by the suspect as indicative of a lack of threat" (2006, 74). While cooperation can certainly indicate a compliant subject with no intent to harm the officer, it is imperative that officers understand there are individuals who will use compliance as a weapon of manipulation. The presence of logical and rational thinking in this profile makes this planning and preparation possible. Someone with contaminated thought is far less likely to maintain the cognitive organization to premediate and organize an attack. As mentioned, when they attack, it is typically impulsive and disorganized.

Clinical Example:

Officers respond to a bar fight. By the time officers arrive, the fight has ended and one of the subjects has remained. As officers approach, the subject is talkative and interactive with officers. He immediately thanks them for their service and states how much he appreciates the police and what they do. He explains the situation and what occurred in a logical and reasonable manner. When officers ask for his identification, he happily provides it. He cooperates with all the officers' questions and his emotional presentation is balanced.

Approach Style:

Individuals in this situation are not in crisis. There is no specific crisis situation with this profile, and it typically represents a calm, compliant citizen. As such, our communication style is going to be task-focused. This means that our communication is for the purpose of accomplishing our police objective. A simple example of this would be asking questions and communicating for the purpose of acquiring information to write a report.

Psychological Status:

Individuals with this profile are typically not experiencing any type of mental illness, and if they do have some type of mental health concern, symptoms are managed and stable. However, if this is an individual who is using the compliant and calm presentation as a manipulation tool, with a negative intention toward the officer, the most likely diagnostic classification would be that of Antisocial

Personality Disorder, or that of someone with traits of psychopathy who is using compliance as a form of psychological manipulation. Individuals with this condition can be very logical and reasonable in their thinking, are typically calm in their emotional presentation, and can be compliant with authority when they are actively engaged in the practice of antisocial acts.

Volatility Risk:

The volatility risk for this profile is considered low. The balance of thought, emotion, and behavior in this profile typically does not cause a volatile response in the individual. This is generally the case, but as mentioned, the officer must always remain mindful of this being used as manipulation, with a sudden escalation in volatility when the individual feels the officer has become vulnerable by letting down psychological defenses.

Volatility Type:

If this individual were to become volatile, specifically in using their compliance as a manipulation tool, the volatility would come in some form of a quick, highly focused, and unprovoked attack. The attack itself would be cognitive. In other words, focused, calm, and purposeful. It would likely follow some assessment of the officer by the individual and premeditation in regard to how the attack would unfold.

Other Behavioral Factors to Consider:

As mentioned, this profile is typically a compliant, cooperative, and engaged citizen. On the other side of the coin, this could also be the presentation of someone who is purposefully using a calm and cooperative demeanor as a tool of manipulation.

CLEAR THOUGHT– LOW EMOTION–NONCOMPLIANT BEHAVIOR

Thought	Emotion	Behavior	Approach Style	Psychological Status	Volatility Risk	Volatility Type	Other Behavioral Factors to Consider
Clear	Low	Noncompliant	Directive comm (clarify limits and make aware of consequences)	Defiant/likely not mentally ill. Purposeful behavior	High risk	Cognitive	Noncompliance is purposeful/ Often anti-police/ Likely criminal minded and antisocial

This combination of thought, emotion, and behavior presents a uniquely concerning combination for officers. The combination of low emotion and noncompliant behavior is typically associated with the demeanor and presentation of a psychopath. These individuals are also not contaminated thinkers and, while often portrayed as "crazy" because of their heinous acts, in reality they are quite logical and intelligent.

The psychopath is an individual who shows a specific cluster of traits in which they are parasitic, manipulative, emotionally disengaged, and unable to experience the typical guilt and remorse experienced by most in our society. Their calculations upon which decisions are made focus specifically on a risk-versus-reward balance, with a strong tendency to avoid risk and experience reward. Their interactions with others are focused on what the individuals can provide to enhance their rewards, and they will use the talents, abilities, and good nature of others for their own benefit, with no true regard for how this may impact the individual. They can be compliant when they believe it is in their best interest, but any compliance is typically a game. They are master provocateurs, able to manipulate others to do their bidding and then stand back and watch everything fall apart. All the while feeling no shame, remorse, or concern related to their actions or how their actions impact others.

The "de-escalation for all" movement, which seemed to gain strength in 2020, has asserted that in every situation where an officer has contact with an individual, de-escalation should be employed. While there are certain profiles for which de-escalation strategies are most appropriate, its potential danger to officers cannot be understated as related to this individual profile. The de-escalation mantra typically directed officers to slow everything down, create time and distance, and try as hard as possible to use communication as an alternative to force. For an individual in crisis, this approach makes sense and is entirely reasonable and necessary. In an individual who is clear-minded, low in emotion, and noncompliant, this is potentially a recipe for disaster.

Our question here is that if someone is void of contaminated thought, meaning they are entirely logical and reasonable in their thinking, and there is no high emotion, then why are they noncompliant? Typically, when we see noncompliance, it is a result of contamination in thinking or in response to high emotion. Its presence, absent of either of these other components, is the hallmark of a psychopath. An individual, who, in the presence of logical thought, and who is not driven by any emotion, remains noncompliant. This is reminiscent of someone who is intentionally noncompliant and purposeful in their resistance. If an officer provides this individual with time and distance, this individual is likely to use that gift as a means of planning ways to escape and/or injure the officer. While the gift of time can be a godsend when used with the right person, it can also be a fatal flaw in decision-making when interacting with this type of person.

Clinical Example:

Officers are dispatched to a man behind a building after the business has closed. Upon making contact, they ask the subject why he is there. He responds, "I am just looking around." When they ask for identification, he refuses. He calmly states that he is not doing anything wrong and is just waiting for a ride. The subject adds, "If you want to arrest me go ahead, but I ain't doing nothing wrong." He then begins discussing the law on trespassing and how he is not violating any laws. He again tells the officers he is waiting for a ride and they have no authority to question him.

Approach Style:

Individuals in this situation are not in crisis. There is no specific crisis situation present and our greater concern is the noncompliance within the context of clear thought and low emotion. In this profile, our goal is to communicate using directive communication. This means the use of communication to show the individual there is a limit to how far he can pursue his behavior and to make him aware of its consequences. By communicating in this manner, we are specifically targeting the psychopath's risk-versus-reward system. By establishing clear boundaries and potential consequences if these boundaries are crossed, we are taking his power of manipulation away and avoiding providing any gifts he can use against us. An individual with this profile will typically quickly recognize the seriousness and legitimacy of the officer, while also recognizing the risks here outweigh any potential reward.

Psychological Status:

Individuals with this profile are likely to show considerable traits of psychopathy. The individual with Antisocial Personality Disorder can also fall into this category as well, but the absence of emotion is the hallmark of the psychopath.

Volatility Risk:

At first glance, one might look at this profile and assume due to the lack of emotion and the absence of contaminated thought, the individual is a low risk. Typically, many in our society, even officers, associate volatility, especially aggression, with emotion. We are inadvertently taught through considerable conditioning that violent or aggressive people are angry people. People in movies don't become violent unless they are angry. In real life, many of the attacks on officers are conducted by rational, calm, focused, and intentional individuals. One of the biggest mistakes people make in assessing someone's risk for violence is to assume that because they are not angry or demonstrating other signs of emotional distress, they will not be aggressive.

Volatility Type:

Any volatility directed toward officers by this individual will be cognitive. While attorneys will attempt to paint this type of person as absent of a guilty mind, in reality, they have a very guilty mind. Meaning, they know exactly what they are doing. When they are volatile, especially in regard to aggressive behavior, their actions are highly organized, targeted, focused, and direct. These are controlled individuals who will quietly kill you without a second thought. This is not the person yelling and screaming while shooting a weapon. This is the individual who, during a traffic stop, calmly reaches between the seats, grabs his gun, and shoots the officer.

Other Behavioral Factors to Consider:

This profile is reminiscent of individuals who are antipolice and who do not typically respect the authority of law enforcement. They can also be classified as "criminally minded," and their goal is going to be to avoid any punishment and to do so at any cost.

CHAPTER IV

APPLICATION FOR THE POLICE TRAINER

For the police trainer interested in applying TEB within the context of de-escalation or crisis intervention training, the application of the TEB is limited only by the creativity of the user. Various trainers around the country have utilized it in different ways and applied it through a variety of different training techniques and venues. However, there are some basic fundamentals of use and application, as well as recommendations of how this instrument may best be applied. In addition, as is the case with all psychological skills training, a process of application is best utilized.

Communicating and effectively intervening with a person in crisis is not an easy task. While some may naturally be more comfortable and/or competent in working within these situations, training is still required. It is akin to defensive tactics. As officers, we understand that defensive tactics must be trained repeatedly and practiced regularly. Without consistent training, when faced with a confrontation, the officer typically resorts back to some primitive form of defense that is not effective. We must train our defensive skills to the point of automaticity so that when they are needed, they are applied with little thought or analysis. It is not the time to think about how to respond when someone swings at us. Rather, it must be instinctive and deeply ingrained in our reflective responses through training. The same is true of communication.

Ironically, while officers seem to understand the need for extensive training in defensive tactics, they are less inclined to view crisis interaction in the same manner. Perhaps this is due to some officers believing it is less fun and certainly not as exciting as defensive tactics training. Regardless, what research tells us related to communication with a person in crisis and the use of complex, sophisticated, and strategically directed communication strategies is that it requires a high cognitive load (Sandi and Pinelo-Nava, 2007) and, thereby, considerable training as well in order to manage that load. This becomes even more critical when considering the arousal levels of the officer during an encounter with a subject in crisis, which can directly impact officer performance (Arble, Daughterty, and Armetz, 2019). Unfortunately, many departments don't give the same weight to training crisis communication and intervention as they do to defensive tactics. While they may be mandated from on high to do some type of training in this area, it is often delivered in the form of "checkbox training," meaning it was done to meet the requirements, but with little detail, vigor, or complexity. This is troubling in that just as defensive tactics are critical in helping an officer go home safely at the end of the shift, so too is their ability to communicate effectively with a person in crisis.

In considering these factors, the recommendations for

training with the TEB model suggest far more than simply obtaining the information. Rather, the information should be applied in high-fidelity training under stress to ensure it can be applied effectively.

Trainers are also strongly encouraged to train the TEB model with tactical training so the two can be cleanly integrated. As mentioned previously, we should not train communication and crisis intervention separate from tactical training. As suggested by Donald Hebb (1949), neurons that fire together wire together. In real life, crisis intervention never occurs in a vacuum. We don't engage in communication to address a person in crisis while ignoring or disengaging from tactical awareness and excellence. Rather, it is done in concert with our tactical awareness in place. Officers are often involved in situations where communication techniques quickly shift into a need for a force response and vice versa. As such, the two must be trained together.

Another reason to train the TEB within the context of tactics is the simple fact that it makes the training more interesting and cognitively challenging. Officers will likely be more invested in training if it is perceived as fun and requires active problem-solving and the potential integration of tactical skills. Just ask any officer, "Would you rather shoot guns or learn about active listening?" Well, you know what the answer would be.

THREE PHASES OF TEB APPLICATION

The TEB can be trained through three specific phases. It is likely the educational and acquisition phases can be done over a day or two, but the practice phase should be prolonged and should continue indefinitely. In other words, consistent practice with the model within simulations/scenario-based training (high-fidelity training) is recommended. The three training phases include:

1. Educational Phase

   In this initial phase, the TEB is introduced to officers and the various elements of the model are discussed. Officers are educated about the fundamental elements of human functioning, with discussions related to thought, emotion, and behavior. Each profile is explained, as are the fundamental elements within each of the profiles.

2. Acquisition Phase

   In this phase, officers are given opportunities to utilize the model in considering various situations and circumstances. This may involve the use of video vignettes where officers are encouraged to apply the model and talk through their assessment of the situation using the various TEB profiles. Socratic questioning about how officers came to their own formulations of the individual profiles and how this would then impact their decisions about intervention should be utilized. Numerous video vignettes focusing on a variety of different profiles should be utilized. Through application in this phase, officers become increasingly familiar with the model and how it works. During this phase, officers are likely going to need to continually reference the TEB profiles to aid in their recall of the various profiles.

3. Practice Phase

> In this phase, officers are given opportunities to work within various scenarios, simulations, and high-fidelity training exercises (scenario-based training) that will allow them to practice the use of the TEB. Through practice, they will begin to understand the model in much greater detail and, through understanding, will not need to rely on rote memory. The practice phase allows the process of transition from using the model as a guide in assessment to the point in which the officer begins to think in terms of the profiles and assess people by considering their thought, emotion, and behavior.

CONCLUSION

Today's police officers are tasked with dealing with the most difficult and challenging individuals within an unstructured and highly dynamic environment. Specific training to enhance skills has been evolving through the years and remains an ever-changing process. While traditional training has focused on what was done in the past and has been carried from generation to generation, recent psychological science and research on human performance has taken a more prominent role.

While the application of psychological science certainly has relevance in the police world, its integration must be done in a manner that is realistic, easily applicable to a police environment, and that, with its implementation, doesn't increase the risk to officer safety. The goal of developing and implementing the TEB model was designed with this in mind. It aims to increase officers' ability to work with human beings in a manner that is not only scientifically sound, but which allows for an easy, realistic transition into the police environment, while also not compromising the necessary police tactics designed to ensure officer safety.

The goal of this book has been to not only increase officer awareness of the basic elements of human functioning—thought, emotion, and behavior—but in expanding characteristics in advancing clinical knowledge. The goal was to do so without relying on complicated, often irrelevant, and overly monolithic diagnostic categories. More importantly, the goal is to advance the science of policing in a manner that not only enhances officers' ability to serve the public, but to do so in a manner that ensures they return safely to their families at the end of each shift.

BIBLIOGRAPHY

The following references were utilized in development of the SOARR model, the TEB model, and completion of this book.

TEXTS AND BOOKS

Asken, Michael, Loren Christenson, and David Grossman. *Warrior Mindset: Mental Toughness Skills for a Nation's Peacekeepers.* 2011.

Charvet, S. Rose. *Words That Change Minds: Mastering the Language of Influence.* Kendall Hunt Publishing, 1997. Second Edition.

Cialdini, Robert. *Influence: The Psychology of Persuasion.* Quill Publications, 1993.

Cialdini, Robert. *Pre-Suasion: A Revolutionary Way to Influence and Persuade.* Simon & Schuster, 2016.

Cloke, Kenneth. *Mediating Dangerously: The Frontiers of Conflict Resolution.* Jossey-Bass Publishers, 2001.

Dimitrius, J. *Reading People: How to Understand People and Predict Their Behavior.* Ballantine Books, 1999.

Hebb, D. O. *The Organization of Behavior: A Neuropsychological Theory.* Wiley, 1949.

Hogan, Kevin. *The Psychology of Persuasion: How to Persuade Others to Your Way of Thinking.* Pelican Publishing, 2003. Fifth Edition.

Kahneman, Daniel. *Thinking, Fast and Slow.* Anchor Canada, 2013. Second Edition.

Lanceley, Frederick. *On-Scene Guide for Crisis Negotiators.* CRC Press, 2003. Second Edition.

Levine, Robert. *The Power of Persuasion: How We're Bought and Sold.* John Wiley & Sons Inc., 2003.

McMains, Michael, and Wayman Mullins. *Crisis Negotiations: Managing Critical Incidents and Hostage Situations in Law Enforcement and Corrections.* Routledge Press, 2015. Fifth Edition.

EMPIRICAL STUDIES

Arble, A., A. Daugherty, and B. Arnetz. "Differential Effects of Physiological Arousal Following Acute Stress on Police Officer Performance in a Stimulated Critical Incident." *Frontiers in Psychology* 10, article 759 (2019): 1–11.

Bosse, T., C. Gerritsen, J. de Man, and S. Tolmeijer. "Adaptive Training for Aggression De-Escalation." In *Artificial Life and Intelligent Agents*, edited by C. Headleand et al. Switzerland: Springer International Publishing, 2015. ALIA 2014. *Communications in Computer and Information Science* 519 (2015): 80–93. DOI: 10.1007/978-3-319-18084-7_7.

Broussard, B., S. Krishan, D. Hankerson-Dyson, and B. D'Orio. "The Police-Based Crisis Intervention Team (CIT) Model: Effects on Officers' Knowledge, Attitudes and Skills." *Psychiatric Services* 65, no. 4 (April 2014): 517–522.

Dysterheft, J., W. Lewinski, D. Seefeldt, and R. Pettit. "The Influence of Start Position, Initial Step Type and

Usage of a Focal Point on Sprinting Performance." *International Journal of Exercise Science* 6, no. 4 (2013): 320–327.

Ewington, J. "Best Practices for Reducing the Use of Coercive Measures." In *The Use of Coercive Measures in Forensic Psychiatric Care: Legal, ethical, and practical challenges*, edited by B. Vollm and N. Nedopil, 285–314. Cham, Switzerland: Springer International Publishing, 2016.

Frohlich, D., F. Rabenschlag, S. Schoppmann, S. Borgwardt, U. Lang, and C. Huber. "Positive Effects of an Anti-Aggression and De-Escalation Training on Ward Atmosphere and Subjective Safety May Depend on Previous Training Experience." *Frontiers in Psychiatry* 9 (2018).

Fyfe, James. "Policing the Emotionally Disturbed." *Journal of the American Academy of Psychiatry and the Law* 28 (2000): 345–347.

Gross, J. "Emotion regulation in adulthood: Timing is Everything." *Current Directions in Psychological Science* 10, no. 6 (2001): 214–219.

Hasselt, V., M. Baker, S. Romano, K. Schlessinger, M. Zucker, R. Dragone, and A. Perera. "Crisis Negotiation Training: A Preliminary Evaluation of Program Efficacy." *Criminal Justice and Behavior* 33, no. 1 (2006): 56–69.

Honig, A., and W. Lewinski. "A Survey of the Research on Human Factors Related to Lethal Force Encounters: Implications for Law Enforcement Training, Tactics and Testimony." *Law Enforcement Executive Forum* 8, no. 4 (2008).

Johnson, David, Joseph Cesario, and Timothy Pleskac. "How Prior Information and Police Experience Impact Decisions to Shoot." *American Psychological Association* 115, no. 4 (2018): 601–623.

Kavanagh, E. L. "A Cognitive Model of Firearms Policing." *Journal of Police and Criminal Psychology* 21, no. 2.

Lavelle, M., S. Duncan, K. James, M. Richardson, L. Renwick, G. Brennan, and L. Bowers. "Predictors of Effective De-Escalation in Acute Inpatient and Psychiatric Settings." *Journal of Clinical Nursing* 25 (2016): 2180–2188.

Lewinski, W., and C. Redmann. "New Developments in Understanding the Behavioral Science Factors in the 'Stop Shooting' Response." *Law Enforcement Executive Forum* 9, no. 4 (2009).

Lewinski, W., J. Dysterheft, N. Dicks, and R. Pettit. "The Influence of Officer Equipment and Protection on Short Sprinting Performance." *Applied Ergonomics* 47 (2015): 65–71.

Lewinski, W., J. Dysterheft, D. Seefeldt, and R. Pettit. "The Influence of Officer Positioning on Movement During a Threatening Traffic Stop Scenario." *Law Enforcement Executive Forum* 13, no. 1 (2013).

Lewinski, W., J. Dysterheft, J. Bushey, and N. Dicks. "Ambushes Leading Cause of Officer Fatalities: When Every Second Counts – Analysis of Officer Movement from Trained Ready Tactical Positions." *Law Enforcement Executive Forum* 15, no. 1 (2015).

Lewinski, W., R. Avery, J. Dysterheft, N. Dicks, and J.

Bushey. "The Real Risks During Deadly Police Shootouts: Accuracy of the Naïve Shooter." *International Journal of Police Science and Management* 17, no. 2 (2015): 117–127.

Miller, Laurence. "Suicide by Cop: Causes, Reactions and Practical Intervention Strategies." *International Journal of Emergency Mental Health* 8: 165–174.

Mohandie, K., and J. Reid Meloy et al. "Suicide by Cop Among Officer Involved Shooting Cases." *Journal of Forensic Science* 54, no. 2 (March 2019).

Mullins, Wayman C. "Advanced Communication Techniques for Hostage Negotiators." *Journal of Police Crisis Negotiations* 2, no. 1 (2002): 63–81.

Noesner, G., and M. Webster. "Crisis Intervention: Using Active Listening Skills in Negotiations." FBI Law Enforcement Bulletin (1997).

Pinizzotto, A., and E. Davis. "Killed in the Line of Duty." Uniform Crime Reports Section, FBI: September 1992.

Pinizzotto, A., E. Davis, and C. Miller. "In The Line of Fire: Violence Against Law Enforcement." Criminal Justice Information Services Division, FBI: October 1997.

Pinizzotto, A., E. Davis, and C. Miller. "Violent Encounters: A Study of Felonious Assault on Our Nations Law Enforcement Officers." Criminal Justice Information Services Division, FBI: August 2006.

Price, O., and J. Baker. "Key Components of De-Escalation Techniques: A Thematic Synthesis." *International Journal of Mental Health Nursing* 21 (2012): 310–319.

Redelmeier, D., and R. Cialdini. "Problems for Clinical Judgement: 5 Principles of influence in Medical Practice." *Canadian Medical Association Journal* 166, no. 13 (2002): 1680–1684.

Reid Meloy, J., J. Hoffman, A. Guldimann, and D. James. "The Role of Warning Behaviors in Threat Assessment: An Exploration and Suggested Typology." *Behavioral Science and the Law* (2011). DOI: 10.1002/bsi.999.

Richmond, J., J. Berlin, A. Fishkind, G. Holloman, S. Zeller, M. Wilson, M. Rifai, and A. Ng. "Verbal De-Escalation of the Agitated Patient: Consensus Statement of the American Association for Emergency Psychiatry Project BETA De-Escalation Workgroup." *Western Journal of Emergency Medicine* 13, no. 1 (2012).

Ross, D. L. "Assessing Lethal Force Liability Decisions and Human Factors Research." *Law Enforcement Executive Forum* 13, no. 2 (2013).

Roy, H., N. Wasylyshyn et al. "Linking Emotional Reactivity Between Laboratory Tasks and Immersive Environments Using Behavior and Physiology." *Frontiers in Human Neuroscience* 13, article 54 (February 2019).

Sandi, C., and M. T. Pinelo-Nava. "Stress and Memory: Behavioral Effects and Neurobiological Mechanisms." *Neural Plasticity* (2007): 1–20. DOI: 10.1155/2007/78970.

Schlosser, M., and M. Gahan. "Police Use of Force: A Descriptive Analysis of Illinois Police Officers." *Law Enforcement Executive Forum* 15, no. 2 (2015).

Todak, N., and L. James. "A Systematic Social Observation Study of Police De-Escalation Tactics." *Police Quarterly* 21, no. 4 (2018): 509–543.

Vecchi, G. M. "Active Listening: The Key to Effective Crisis Negotiation." *ACR Crisis Negotiation News* 1 (2003): 4–6.

Vecchi, G. M. "Hostage/Barricade Management: A Hidden Conflict Within Law Enforcement." *FBI Law Enforcement Bulletin* 71 (2002): 1–6.

Vecchi, G. M., V. Van Hasselt, and S. Romano. "Crisis (hostage) Negotiations: Current Strategies in High Risk Conflict Resolution." *Aggression and Violent Behavior* 10 (2005): 533–551.

Vickers, J. and W. Lewinski. "Performing Under Pressure: Gaze Control, Decision Making and Shooting Performance of Elite and Rookie Police Officers." *Human Movement Science* (2012): 101–117.

Violanti, J., and J. Drylie. "Copicide." *Journal of Police Criminal Psychology* 25 (2010):125–126.

Yu, Rongjun. "Stress Potentiates Decision Biases: A Stress Induced Deliberation-to-Intuition (SIDI) Model." *Neurobiology of Stress* 3 (2016): 83–95.

ARTICLES

Aveni, Thomas. "The Must Shoot vs. May Shoot Controversy." *Law and Order.* January 2005.

Butler, Chris. "Strategic Communications: Calgary Police Service Applied Basic Curriculum." February 2001.

Daigle, Eric. "Is More Training Really the Answer?" Daigle Law Group, LLC. IACP Legal Officer Section in *Police Chief Magazine.* March 2016.

Daigle, Eric. "Use of Force and Mental Illness: Policy Development for No-Win Situations." Daigle Law Group, LLC. 2018. www.daiglelawgroup.com.

Golden, Jeffrey. "De-escalating Juvenile Aggression." *Police Chief Magazine.* May 2004.

"An Integrated Approach to De-Escalation and Minimizing Use of Force." Police Executive Resource Forum. August 2012.

King, Brendan. "Calm Every Storm: Preventing Aggressive Behavior With Your Words." Crisis Consultant Group, LLC. 2015.

Miller, Laurence. "Suicide by Cop: Prevention, Response & Recovery." Practical Police Psychology—PoliceOne. March 18, 2007. https://www.policeone.com/police products/communications/crisis-communications/articles/1228463-Suicide-by-cop-Prevention response-and-recovery/.

Pinizzotto, A., and E. Davis. "Offenders Perceptual Shorthand: What Messages are Law Enforcement Officers Sending to Offenders?" FBI Law Enforcement Bulletin. June 1999.

Pinizzotto, A., E. Davis, and C. Miller. "Officers Perceptual Shorthand: What Messages are Offenders Sending to Law Enforcement Officers?" FBI Law Enforcement Bulletin. July 2000.

"Rightful Policing." New Perspectives in Policing. Harvard Kennedy School & NIJ. February 2015.

Salvatore, Tony. "Suicide by Cop: Broadening Our Understanding." FBI Law Enforcement Bulletin. September 9, 2014. https://leb.fbi.gov/articles/featured-articles/suicide-by-cop-broadening-our understanding.

San Francisco Police Department Crisis Intervention Team Annual Report (2023, 2022, 2021, 2020).

Wallentine, Ken. "Should I Stay or Should I Go?" *Police Magazine*. October 16, 2017.

ABOUT THE AUTHOR

John Azar-Dickens, PhD, is a licensed clinical psychologist whose practice specialty is in the area of forensic and police psychology. In July of 2011, Dr. Azar-Dickens completed the Basic Officer Mandate Program through Georgia POST and was sworn in as a police officer with the City of Rome, Georgia, Police Department in August of 2011. He presently works as a patrol officer within the special operations unit for the department.

Dr. Azar-Dickens is employed as a forensic psychologist with the Georgia Department of Behavioral Health and Developmental Disabilities and maintains a private practice in the area of forensic and police psychology.

He has been a partnering instructor with Force Science since 2012 and has conducted training for law enforcement around the United States and Canada in areas of human performance, de-escalation, and officer wellness.

www.ingramcontent.com/pod-product-compliance
Lightning Source LLC
Chambersburg PA
CBHW071721020426
42333CB00017B/2350